Pelican Books
Clever Children in Comprehensive Schools

Auriol Stevens has been Education Correspondent for the *Observer* since 1978. Born in 1940 in Lancashire, she read history at Somerville College, Oxford, and social studies at London University. She worked as a freelance journalist in the United States, London and West Germany, and joined the staff of *The Times Educational Supplement* in 1972, becoming deputy editor in 1975.

Aurial Stevens is married and has three children.

Auriol Stevens

Clever Children in
Comprehensive Schools

Penguin Books

Penguin Books Ltd, Harmondsworth,
Middlesex, England
Penguin Books, 625 Madison Avenue,
New York, New York 10022, U.S.A.
Penguin Books Australia Ltd, Ringwood,
Victoria, Australia
Penguin Books Canada Ltd, 2801 John Street,
Markham, Ontario, Canada L3R 1B4
Penguin Books (N.Z.) Ltd, 182–190 Wairau Road,
Auckland 10, New Zealand

First published 1980

Made and printed in Great Britain by
Richard Clay (The Chaucer Press) Ltd,
Bungay, Suffolk
Set in Linotype Baskerville

Contents

17

Acknowledgements

My thanks to all who gave up time to talk to me; to all who let me tramp about their schools; to Harry Judge and Stuart Maclure for reading early drafts with a critical eye; to my employers, past and present, for giving me time to get the job done; and to my family, who put up with it all nobly.

Introduction

Four out of five secondary school children in this country now go to comprehensive schools. Thirty years ago, clever children were singled out early in their lives to be taught separately from other children in schools designed specifically to nurture their academic potential. Even ten years ago, more than half of all children went through this early sorting process. But now most children go on together from primary school to common secondary schools. The sorting goes on inside the schools instead of between them and the process is stretched out over the whole of a child's secondary school career.

The purpose of this book is to examine the effects of this fundamental change upon clever children. It is widely believed that they have suffered; that they are being held back academically in these common schools; that, in the cause of social justice, excellence has been sacrificed. The belief is apparent among politicians, teachers, administrators, school inspectors, commentators, above all among parents.

Some, who are rich enough to have a choice, decide, often at considerable personal sacrifice, to pay for private schooling rather than risk their children's academic future in the hurly-burly of the common schools. 'I just want her to have a decent academic education,' has become a cliché among affluent liberal parents. 'We just don't feel we can sacrifice our children to our principles.' In the past, such families might more usually have made the financial sacrifices required to save a child of average intelligence from a secondary modern school. Now that the 11-plus has gone, it is more usual to find people anxious to save a clever child from a comprehensive school.

Many who cannot, or do not, choose to pay for private schooling agonize endlessly over their children's progress, wondering whether indeed those children will turn out to have been sacrificial lambs, whether they will be set at a disadvantage in the rat race of a highly competitive society.

Drawing on published material, on research reports and statistics, on personal interviews and on visits to many private and state schools, I have tried to discover what foundations, if any, in fact exist for this pervasive belief. I have tried to assess the gains and losses of clever children as the school system has been transformed. I have tried, too, to see whether continued contact with the clever has brought any benefits to other children during the secondary school years.

I have concentrated not on the very clever, the tiny minority of exceptionally brilliant children, but on all those who might in other days have expected to clear the early selection hurdles and go to grammar schools. Such children are roughly the top 20 to 25 per cent of the full range of ability. They are all those who get five or more passes at GCE Ordinary (O-) level (or the equivalent). They are all those who take Advanced (A-) level exams and all those who go on from school to become full-time students in higher education. They are those who, on standard intelligence tests, produce the long tapering tail at the right-hand end of the typical bell-shaped curve (as shown in the accompanying figure).

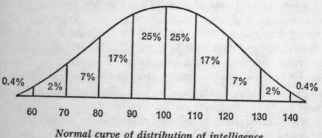

Normal curve of distribution of intelligence.

The GCE exams are primarily designed for these children. O-level is theoretically designed for the most able 20 per cent in each subject, and though many more than 20 per cent of all children in practice pass O-level in a few subjects, it is, indeed, only a quarter who achieve five or more passes at this level. Only 16 per cent pass one or more A-level subjects. Only 14 per cent go on to study full-time in higher education.

In trying to establish what has been happening to these cleverer children as schools have changed, I have made considerable use of exam statistics, higher education admission figures and intelligence test scores. I am aware of the dangers. Intelligence tests are many and varied. The content and the methods and scales of scoring differ. The same children perform differently on different tests. Tests themselves are subject to all kinds of biases. But, for all their limitations, such tests do provide the best indication available of the raw material on which a school is working. Without some such guide it is impossible to tell how well a school is doing by its pupils.

Examination statistics, too, are open to objection. There is no such thing as a fixed standard. Many of the things that are important in education are not measured by examinations. Many cannot be quantified at all in any objective form. But exams do provide a generally accepted if imperfect yardstick against which children's academic performance can be measured, a way of checking the end product of schools' endeavours.

Figures for admission to higher education are a still more unreliable guide. Motivation, as well as qualifications, determines young people's actions when they plan their future. But, again, such measures have their uses. Success and status in our society are coming increasingly to depend on a high level of qualification. The schools must pass on young people adequately prepared to undertake further training at the highest levels and willing to master the complex skills required by a modern society.

For all the drawbacks and all the dryness, figures do provide a more useful indication of what is happening in schools than can be got by simply relying on subjective judgements. Whether these judgements take the form of considered views expressed in measured terms by experienced teachers and by school inspectors, or whether they are the stuff of local gossip in the laundrette or the pub, or over private dinner tables, they need constant checking against such objective measures as exist.

But I have drawn on subjective judgements too: my own and those of just such others as I have mentioned. I have sat in classes and in meetings, talked to children, to parents, to teachers. I have looked at children's work and at their teachers' comments on it, trying to get some idea of the standards reached, the work covered and the teachers' expectations of their pupils. I have looked at the same subjects taught to the same age groups in different types of schools and in different schools of the same type.

It proved a tricky business. Journalists are not trusted and teachers are understandably wary of exposing either their pupils or themselves to unknown outsiders. The work I have been shown has, as a result, been in most instances work of which that school was proud, the work of teachers who were confident. The classes I have sat in have been those of teachers who did not mind the presence of an observer. I can make no claim that what I have seen is typical. It is safe to assume that it was often the best.

It rapidly became apparent that generalization about types of school was extremely difficult since the variation between schools of one kind was often as great as the variation between schools of different kinds. But the undertaking was no less valuable for that, and the difficulties should not detract from my gratitude to all those who did give me the run of their schools. I hope none will feel I have abused their hospitality nor that I have breached the undertaking given to all that no school I visited would be identified.

1 Eroded Differentials

Comprehensive schools by definition favour most those who lost most under the previous selective system. Simply to remove selection tests removes from 80 per cent of the population the certainty of failure at the age of eleven. Children who would have failed their 11-plus tests attend schools where the average ability is automatically higher than it would have been in a secondary modern; where expectations may also be higher and where a wider range of opportunities is kept open.

There is no such automatic gain for children who, under the old system, would have passed the tests. On the contrary, they now find themselves in schools where the average is automatically lower and where the teachers have a whole range of preoccupations they did not have in grammar schools. It is only reasonable to suppose that, unless the new comprehensive schools make a particular effort to ensure that the cleverer children are not dragged down, the performance of those children will be less good than it might have been.

Unfortunately, since the late 1960s, as comprehensive reorganization has gathered pace, circumstances have been such as to make that extra concentration a lower priority than others, not least the simple need to survive from day to day. Such time as there was for extra attention has in most cases been used to help make school appeal to the lost sheep of earlier generations. In the first place, the schools have been faced with constant change as a consequence of reorganisation and expansion of the secondary school population.

In 1965, the Labour government sent a circular letter (Circular 10/65) to all local education authorities asking them to submit plans for ending selection. Some authorities were already doing this, and throughout the 1960s the pace of change quickened. In 1974, the upheaval, which was already considerable, was made worse by the reorganization of local government along lines laid down in the 1972 Local Government Act. This threw the education authorities responsible for the schools into the melting-pot. Boundary changes brought disparate local arrangements together; conflicting patterns of organization had to be ironed out; and, in some areas, all this meant a second round of school reorganization.

At the same time there has been a constant battle with local pressure-groups to protect particular schools. Such campaigns, often successful, have nearly always been mounted in defence of grammar schools, very rarely of secondary moderns. The comprehensive system which has been introduced against this background is therefore lopsided and incomplete. In 1978 (according to *Education*, 1 September 1978), 59 out of 104 local authorities still maintained some grammar schools. Although by then over four fifths of all state school children (roughly the same proportion as used to go to secondary moderns) were said to be in comprehensive schools, 7 per cent, approaching half the rest, were in grammar schools. Another 6 per cent of children were in mainly selective independent and direct grant schools. Quite apart from administrative upheaval, the new comprehensives have had to fight an uphill battle for acceptance. If they have not yet won this battle where the parents of cleverer children are concerned, it has not prevented them from being judged as if they had had their full share of those clever children, where many are in fact little more than renamed secondary moderns.

Judging fairly the performance of the schools is still very difficult. Nearly half the existing comprehensives were still to see a full generation through to eighteen in 1978. As a result of this newness, it was not possible to find a local authority which has been fully comprehensive long enough for changes in numbers going to university to become apparent. Some had grammar and direct grant schools in the area, or had until recently. In some, the boundaries of the authority had changed. In others, the change to comprehensive schools was too recent.

These, then, are not settled schools. They are often in a

motley collection of buildings scattered over a large area. They are still staffed by many teachers who were hired originally to do a different job in a different school. They often still contain groups of children who were at eleven told they were sheep or goats.

On top of this, they have had to take in growing numbers. Between 1968 and 1977 (the year in which the school population reached its all-time peak), the number of school children in England grew by 20 per cent from just over seven million to more than eight and a half million. The school leaving age was raised to sixteen and the number of under fives in school went up from 230,000 to 415,000.

Expansion put pressure on the supply of teachers throughout the 1960s and 1970s. And, apart from general shortages, there have long been and are still shortages in central subjects such as maths, French, science and crafts. In the early 1970s the shortages, combined with low pay, produced a merry-go-round of teachers pursuing promotion. Over the country as a whole in 1972, 9.5 per cent of teachers left the profession and another 11 per cent moved school. In some inner cities, a quarter of the teachers left their schools in 1973.

Teachers were constantly on the move; the average time spent in one school was short. Many teachers were relatively new to the job. In 1973, as the merry-go-round reached its fastest spin, over 40,000 new teachers completed their training. They represented a very high proportion of those who had applied to the training institutions. In those years, applications barely out-numbered acceptances, and most of those who entered courses qualified. There was little scope for selection, either by trainers or by employers, and while many candidates were good teacher material, others were inevitably less so. A fair number were taken on in schools even if they did not have the specialism needed, any pair of hands being better than none.

The teaching force increased by 50 per cent between 1966 and 1977. Yet, despite the scramble, the percentage of entrants to teaching who have A-levels has steadily increased. In 1977, over 80 per cent had one A-level, nearly 60 per cent had two.

From 1980, every entrant to teaching will need two. The proportion of graduates among state school teachers as a whole has also risen. One teacher in six was a graduate in 1946–7, one in five in 1970, one in four in 1976.

Despite shortages, the pupil–teacher ratio in schools has edged down from 28 to 1 in primary schools and 18·4 to 1 in secondary schools in 1966 to 23·6 to 1 in primary schools and 16·9 to 1 in secondary schools in 1978. It has been no mean achievement.

Shortages and expansion gave the teachers the lever which they needed in the early 1970s to bargain for higher pay. They were able to demonstrate a serious fall in their relative position in the earnings league. Even so, an aggressive campaign was needed to get their case taken seriously. Much play was made of the difficulty of teachers' work. The high turnover of teachers in city schools was blamed both on stress and on property prices beyond the reach of teachers on their current salaries.

Schools all over the country, and particularly in London, were disrupted by teachers' strikes. Children were sent home and both day-to-day teaching and the teachers' public image were gravely damaged. The picture which teachers painted of the stresses and strains of their work – the cry of 'stinking fish' – so as to back their claim for a decent wage, was taken by the public as evidence that the schools were dreadful. This damage outlasted the disruption.

The settlements recommended by the Houghton Committee in 1974, together with substantial increases in the London allowance, improved the financial rewards of school teaching. At the same time it became apparent that the numbers of children in schools were going to fall. The birthrate turned downwards in 1964, and continued every year to decline more rapidly than expected until 1978, when it showed signs of a slight upturn. In the 1970s there was a sudden, belated rush to turn off the taps of teacher supply. The painful business of cutting back the institutions which had mushroomed to cope with the shortages culminated in the wave of closures announced in 1977. But the taps were not turned off soon enough to avoid the creation of a pool of trained but unemployed teachers – over 9,200 of them in 1979. This, for the first time since the 1930s, put schools in the happy position of being able to pick and choose their recruits.

Stability returned to the teaching force only in the mid 1970s. The children whose exam results are so far recorded in published statistics are therefore those who have suffered from the worst chaos of both reorganization and teacher turnover.

The second major factor limiting the schools' capacity to give attention to their bright pupils is that organization into comprehensive schools has coincided with – indeed, is part of – rapid social change which is producing all sorts of conflicting pressures.

Inflation has done more in recent years to erode inequalities of income than have decades of redistributive taxation. Letters to *The Times* have regularly charted the decline in purchasing power of higher salaries. Many families who would in earlier generations have sent their children to independent schools without a second thought cannot now afford the fees. This is particularly so because inflation has also driven independent school fees up to an average of well over £2,000 a year for boarding places and £1,000 for day places for boys. (It is somewhat less for girls.) This was an increase of around 80 per cent compared with September 1974 (Independent Schools Information Service Survey (ISIS) figures, 1978).

The direct grant schools, cut off by the Labour government from their subsidy in 1976, mostly became independent, though their fees have remained in many cases lower than other independent schools. The grammar schools have been disappearing. The result of these changes is that more of the privileged members of society are now sending their children to the common schools, where they make anxious and demanding clients. They want exam passes, credentials which will ensure that their children do not lose their place on the social ladder. They want to be assured that, in choosing the local comprehensive, they are not jeopardizing their children's futures.

These families are only part of the comprehensive school's clientèle. K. R. Fogelman in *Britain's Sixteen Year Olds*, the third in a series of studies which followed up all the children born in one week in 1958, gives a broader picture. More than a quarter of the children claimed never to read a book outside school. In every hundred, eight had no bed of their own, nine had been in trouble with the police, more than thirteen were not living with their father. Over half admitted to truanting. One pair of parents in five was said by teachers to take no interest in their children's education. None of this has meant that the schools are spared pressure through indifference. One parent in three, Fogelman found, was in some degree dissatisfied with his or her child's school. The most frequent complaints were lack of discipline and lack of hard work or 'stretching', followed by 'low standards', high teacher turnover and indifference to the children. Unemployment and the rising level of skill demanded by employers has sharpened such parental anxiety. Nearly a third of sixteen- and seventeen-year-olds were unemployed in July 1977, compared with one in eight in July 1975.

At the same time, social values are changing. In Avon, a group of secondary teachers and education officials together drafted a report in 1977 on growing social pressures. Among those they listed were broken marriages, trivia and violence in the media, lax law enforcement, working mothers and crumbling moral values – 'Sex is treated as an end in itself, obscenity is free expression, dishonesty is only self-help.' It was expected, the report said, that, 'In an increasingly violent, dishonest, vandalistic and immoral society, our schools should be temples of pure thought, speech and action.' One of the heads at that meeting has seen, in twenty years, the percentage of maladjusted children in his school – using the same assessment test – rise from 2 to 23 per cent.

For the first time in this country, schools now contain children who are ambitious, bored, sick, clever, average, dim and naughty, rich and poor all under one roof. For every parent demanding more homework, schools can produce examples of parents complaining that, 'I'm not having my child doing overtime.' They are expected somehow to meet the needs and aspirations of all of them without manifest unfairness and to turn out the sort of citizens society would like to have rather than replicas of those it already has.

For schools, these pressures mean immensely hard, detailed work trying to reconcile conflicting claims for attention. It is not surprising that the most strident are dealt with first. In one inner city comprehensive, the equivalent of four teachers' time is occupied in dealing with troublesome children, with social workers and with the juvenile courts.

In many schools, special units are being set up as a way of getting disruptive children out of classrooms so that others can learn: a matter of increasing urgency as demands for higher standards grow. One school I visited kept a room for this purpose, permanently staffed by teachers who gave up their free periods voluntarily to do it. Another had appointed a senior teacher as full-time supervisor of a separate class. In yet another, one of three deputy heads did no teaching. She was in charge of the school's pastoral care and might sometimes spend a whole day talking to three children.

In 1979, Her Majesty's Inspectorate published two reports on the ways in which schools cope with disruptive children. *Truancy and Behavioural Problems in Some Urban Schools* and *Behavioural Units*. The first concentrated on general school practice, the second on special units for the disruptive. Many schools, they found, were turning against separate units, the vogue idea of the mid 1970s, and were achieving considerable success with difficult children by means of careful school organization and planning. This success was often a result of the personality and energy of particular teachers.

The time and energy of outstanding teachers who could be teaching the bright and well behaved is concentrated instead in many schools upon the most delinquent. The bright and well behaved gain indirectly by having the disrupters removed from their lessons, but, in the process, they miss out on the stimulation those senior teachers could provide.

Some of the children who benefit from this sort of special attention will be clever. There is enough research evidence to show that unidentified talent can lead to misbehaviour – for example, in Mia Kellmer Pringle's study, *Able Misfits* (1970).

And there is evidence that in certain cases trouble is of the school's not the home's making; that the naughtiness of some clever children is caused by the school's failure to realize their ability and give them sufficiently exacting academic work, as M. E. Lonascher and N. P. C. Cavanagh have commented in an article in the *British Medical Journal* (1977, No. 2).

This is much more likely to happen to the children of the poor, many of them black, than it is to children born into more privileged sections of society where intellectual ability is highly valued. Many of these underestimated children would probably not in the past have gone to grammar schools, and their chances of doing well should, at least in theory, be enhanced in comprehensives. But there is still the same risk that they will be submerged among the numerous socially handicapped children who are not particularly clever.

The extent of social handicap is so great in some schools that it is hard for teachers to disentangle what behaviour is a consequence of which cause. Some inner city schools have large numbers of immigrant children, many of whom do not speak much English. Language barriers then make it still harder to assess ability. Even though schools with many disadvantaged pupils are often generously staffed with, in some cases, one teacher to thirteen or fourteen pupils, the task is such that the clever are liable to be neglected if they are not actually delinquent. Certainly they will not get the attention they would receive in a similarly staffed independent school, or even in a rather less generously staffed grammar school. It is little wonder if parents continue to believe that the bright and well behaved get more attention in fee-paying schools, especially when these are compared with comprehensives in areas of multiple social deprivation.

A third factor which has limited what comprehensives can do for their cleverer pupils has, since the mid 1970s, been strict financial restraint. The first wave of cuts came in the mid 1950s, just as schools began to realize that the interests of the bright, well-adjusted pupils did in fact need particular attention.

Spending on schools has risen in real terms since 1965 by over 70 per cent, while the number of young people at school has risen by about 20 per cent. But the days of growing spending, like the days of growing numbers, are over. Even before the Conservatives came to power in May 1979, it had changed.

In order to control a disturbingly high rate of inflation and to ensure adequate resources for regenerating industry, the Government's top two priorities, economic restraint has been necessary. It has been reflected most sharply in the reduction of public expenditure since 1975. Education in company with other programmes such as housing and roads has had to take its share of these cuts amounting in the period 1975 to 1977 to £150 million (2·4%).

This was the bald statement made in the Labour government's 1977 Green Paper, *Education in Schools*. The blanket statement covered cuts made through the rate support grant (the annual government grant to local government which covers about 60 per cent of their spending), particularly in the counties. These amounted in some places to as much as a seventh of their treasury grant in a single year.

Furthermore, education, as the largest item in local government budgets, had not met with much sympathy in certain areas when it came to cutting back on spending. Oxfordshire, Cambridgeshire, Essex, Northamptonshire, Kent and Surrey were among those which lopped large sums of money off their education budgets in real terms. This had already meant, in some areas, closing libraries; cutting back on books, equipment and materials; hiring less teachers for more children; dismissing large numbers of part-time teachers and non-teaching ancillaries. Some local authorities, worried by the government's imposition of cash limit (a refusal to bail out local authorities who overspend), underspent even on the reduced targets set by the government. The figures have been the subject of much dispute, but underspending of £200 million on education between 1976 and 1978 is the most usual sum quoted.

In 1976–7, according to figures given in *The Times Educational Supplement* for 18 November 1977, spending on books dropped in real terms to 80 per cent of the 1971–2 level in secondary schools. Buckinghamshire, for example, cut its school library service book fund from £85,490 in 1976–7 to £19,660 for 1977–8. Capitation money (the cash allowance schools get for each pupil) has been frozen or in some places even cut. At the same time, the cost of essentials such as paper and exercise books has gone up. The prices of materials needed for craft work and for science – wood, metal, cooking materials, chemicals – have gone up. In late 1978, there were small signs of recovery, but this rapidly changed with the election of the Conservative government. Three per cent was promptly cut from the budget for 1979–80, a year which had already begun. Further substantial cuts were announced for subsquent years. For the first time, redundancies became a real possibility.

The extent of the damage to education from recent spending cuts is not known. There are no national figures nor, in any case, are such things readily quantifiable. Agitation from the teachers' official organizations, because, like good trade unionists, their first priority has been jobs, has concentrated more on the threat to people than the threat to materials.

The unions have done a great deal to ensure that local authorities do not cut back too far on teaching staff. They have done much less to protect cash allowances, library grants and money for building maintenance. Nor have they campaigned as fiercely as they might have done for extra clerical and other ancillary help. In Nottinghamshire, the education committee, on which teachers are represented, agreed to cuts in capitation allowances and the county library grant, in ancillary help and money for maintenance of buildings and playing fields, amounting to some £800,000 for 1979–80. In exchange, 175 teaching jobs which would otherwise have been axed were saved.

In practical terms, the problems in schools are serious. When, in 1979, schools were closed because the caretakers were on strike, one secondary school head in the London borough of Barking realized abruptly how short his school was of textbooks. It would, he reckoned, have cost between £6,000 and £10,000 to buy enough books for all the children to be able to take home work while the school remained shut..

These kinds of shortages are particularly important for clever children, since they are most able to work on their own given adequate materials. They also get through books faster and use more of them.

Nor are books the only problem. Take, as an example, a physics teacher instructing an A-level group in School A, a large mixed-sex comprehensive. The experiment they were doing wouldn't work, and trying to get it right delayed a very fast group. 'I came here from an independent school,' the teacher said later. 'There we had twelve technicians for twelve labs. Here we have three for twelve labs. There that experiment would have worked.'

Pupil–teacher ratios, taken overall, are not very much worse in the state secondary schools than they are in the private sector. Inflation has seen to that. Class sizes, too, can be very similar, particularly during the two years leading up to public exams. The wide range of subjects offered in many comprehensives produces relatively small teaching groups in each. Independent schools, with their more homogeneous population, tend to offer fewer choices and therefore to teach O-level subjects in comparatively large groups.

Those who do worst are the middle schools, schools which take children from eight or nine until twelve or thirteen. The two I visited, Schools B and C, both transferred children to high school at thirteen. One of them, School B, had a staffing ratio of 1:22 and was keeping very quiet about it since the staffing standard for middle schools in that particular local authority was 1:26. The other school, School C, was being held strictly to a ratio of 1:26 by its very different local education authority.

The difference between what the two schools were able to do for their fastest children was marked and was attributed in both cases to staffing. In School B, the extra teachers meant that fast groups in this 'gin and Jag belt' school were taken out to do extra work: Shakespeare, poetry, maths. There was little need for comparable remedial groups, since 60–80 per cent of the children would probably have passed the 11-plus in the days of selection. 'We don't have non-readers coming to us at all,' the head said. Nor did they have the time-wasting and expensive problems over missing pencils and exercise books and 'shrinking' library stock which drain the resources of both cash and patience in more fraught schools.

This head was, as a result, able to send his staff off on courses for the teaching of the gifted. He had even recently found one lot of parents complaining that their children were getting too much homework. It was quite a change from the school's early days when the staff were subjected to abuse from parents for low standards.

'The staff have been thoroughly frightened by some of it. These are the sort of people who don't beat their wives with their fists, they do it with words. We find we have to stand between them and their children sometimes. They can be over-ambitious and the children crumple a bit.'

The decision to pay more attention to the able was not taken without prolonged agonizing in the staff room over whether this was the right use of resources. And the policy's survival was in doubt. The head did not expect to keep his extra teachers long.

The other middle school, School C, was less well staffed because its local authority had decided that sixteen to nineteen-year-olds in the county should be given priority in the distribution of resources. Improving staffing in middle schools had been postponed.

The school achieved wonders in terms of music and craft-work with its 400 children. It had an eighty-strong orchestra and an eighty-strong recorder and guitar group. It had its own internal radio station built and manned by the children. The standard, particularly of the pottery, was startling. But the academic work showed signs of deprivation at the top (see page 89).

'We do withdraw two or three children for extra maths and the science department have a faster top set. We could do more but we simply haven't the staff. The slower ones get more resources: it's the only chance they'll get,' the headmaster said.

The draconian cuts announced in 1979 cannot help but

affect what is offered to the clever. Savings of the kind required are impossible without worsening staffing ratios since staff account for around two thirds of all education spending. One of the first things to go will be extra provision for the faster learning children.

In day-to-day terms, the implications for the bright children of structural changes in the schools and local authorities, of the multifarious pressures on schools and of severe spending limits, can be seen in the case of School D, a mixed-sex school in the north-east which takes children from thirteen to eighteen.

As a grammar school, it used to have a fast stream who took O-levels early and then spent three years in the sixth form leading to the Oxford and Cambridge entrance exams. In 1978 that group had gone. Greek had gone. Russian had gone. Latin was confined to the sixth form. The top O-level streams were taught in groups of thirty-two for the main compulsory subjects, and the groups for option subjects for O-level were going up from between twenty or twenty-five to around twenty-eight or twenty-nine.

This was done to make it possible for the three lowest ability classes to have only twenty in each and for each group to be taught by two teachers working together. The school's timetable for thirteen-year-olds showed that sixty children in the bottom forms took up 135 staff periods in a week while ninety children in the top three forms took up 110 staff periods.

Set beside this School E, a boys' public school which had a small bottom remedial group of about ten. With careful coaching and encouragement at the hands of a particularly skilled teacher, the boys in this group – their IQs would all be above average, around 108 – were nursed through between five and seven O-levels, with some A and B grades. 'It would be quite impossible to do it if there were twenty let alone thirty in the class,' according to the teacher.

Compared with School E – and it is an unfair comparison, since that school and, within it, that teacher was not typical – even a comprehensive which does not have a difficult intake must seem at a disadvantage in what it can offer in academic terms to those with a choice about the sort of school to which they send their children. It would be rare to find a comprehensive which did not have, say, 10 per cent whose reading age was below chronological age and on whom special attention must be lavished. It would not, indeed, be a comprehensive without such children, and without a further group who would take very few public exams. Children with IQs around 100–110 are never going to get, in comprehensive schools where they are above the average, the sort of remedial help provided by School E.

Private schooling of this quality is not, however, available to many. A more useful comparison is therefore with the old selective systems. Children with IQs of 100–110 did not go to grammar schools in most areas of the country. Very roughly 25 per cent of the population falls above an IQ level of 110.

Selection at eleven has been convincingly shown to have been unfair. Alfred Yates and Douglas Pidgeon, in their study, *Admission to Grammar Schools* (1957), suggested that each year as many as 12 per cent, or 78,000 children, were misplaced. Much of the respectability of IQ testing rested on the work of Sir Cyril Burt. Recent revelations about the way in which Burt falsified his evidence have cast further doubts on the reliability of such techniques. And even Burt had warned that IQ tests became progressively less useful as the percentage to be selected grew.

Grammar schools were, in their hey-day, taking between 20 and 25 per cent of the secondary population, though the proportion varied from about 10 to 45 per cent, depending on the number of grammar schools in a particular area. Many of those capable of profiting by academic teaching ended up in secondary moderns. This would have been particularly true of late developers and those whose primary school or home background did not help to produce a good performance on formal tests. It was, indeed, the needs of these children which produced pressure, both for the introduction of CSE exams and a general acceptance that O-level could be taken by secondary modern pupils.

Some secondary modern schools were – and some of the remaining ones still are – extremely good. School F, a secondary modern in a small home counties town where the top 30 per cent of the ability range go to grammar schools, is still such a one. Known as 'the comprehensive' by local parents, it had no pupils with an IQ of over 114 on entry. (This was high for a secondary modern receiving only the lower 70 per cent of children because IQ scores of children in this district were well above the national average. Nationally, 114 would be less than 20 per cent of the way down the ability scale. In many areas, children of this ability would have gone to grammar school.)

Twenty sixth-formers from School F went on to university or polytechnic degree courses in 1978, yet, even with this level of academic success to its credit, the school had needed to bend all its efforts in the first two years to rebuilding confidence shattered by failure in the selection tests.

There was never any guarantee that all secondary moderns would reach this sort of standard. For most of those who would have failed the 11-plus, the comprehensive represents a reprieve from being tagged with failure and assigned to a second-rate school. But for those who would have passed, it represents an erosion of differentials.

Grammar schools are not noticeably less well staffed than comprehensives, unless the comprehensive has generous priority allowances. Indeed, they may be better off if they have a large sixth form in proportion to the size of the school since most education authorities provide more generous staffing for pupils over fifteen or sixteen than for younger ones. The Inner London Education Authority is unusual in staffing all its schools on a ratio basis of 1 : 17 regardless of age.

With such a staffing level, a grammar school will not have to provide special coaching for remedial classes, or teach its pupils English, or staff a sanctuary for the troublesome. It does not have to find ways of providing somehow for all abilities. If a pupil can't cope, they can be – though rarely are – transferred. Not only is the job more straightforward, but in grammar schools a higher proportion of the staff are graduates – around three quarters throughout the period from 1950 to 1974.

In secondary modern schools the number of graduates has been rising steadily, but is still only about 20 per cent. Comprehensives fall, unsurprisingly, in the middle, with 42·9 per cent of their staff being graduates in 1974. Good teachers are not necessarily graduates. Many of the best are not, particularly the women. Women with degrees were relatively rare before the expansion of higher education in the 1960s following the recommendations of the Robbins Report on the future of higher education. Many girls who had the ability to take degrees went instead into teacher training.

Clever children are those who have the capacity, whether or not they choose to do so, to continue their education after school in those institutions which produce graduates. The chance of their aspiring to higher education and the suitability of their preparation for it are likely to be materially assisted by being taught by the products of those institutions. Also, to be less mincing about it, children like to be taught by people expert in their subject, people who have interesting information to impart. A teacher who has studied for a subject degree (and not a B.Ed.) has had access to the sort of information which can stretch those children's minds just as a skilled craftsman can demonstrate skills in a way which raises people's idea of what is possible better than can a competent handyman.

In comprehensives, not only are there fewer graduate teachers than there are in grammar schools, but those teachers, because of social pressures – which grammar and independent schools are largely spared – are often the ones who spend a great deal of their time coping with the most intractable problems. The better qualified they are and the better they teach, the more likely it is that they will be given posts of responsibility. Four out of five comprehensive heads are graduates, as are nearly two thirds of their deputies, their senior teachers and those holding scale five posts.

'Seeing parents and chasing children who haven't done work is taking up so much of my time and energy that my teaching is now probably the worst in the department. My classes are really getting a very poor deal and by the time I get off home, I'm only fit for watching *Crossroads*.'

Thus the head of maths in School G, a not particularly fraught country comprehensive, with some rural poverty, a rather sleepy atmosphere but not the turbulence of some inner city schools. He is not unusual. The best teachers – and one must assume that the head of a department is one of the best – are not only distracted by the bad and lazy, they are exhausted by them too. One group of children in that particular school is credited with having put three teachers into hospital in its time.

There is still another counter-claim to that of the clever on such teachers. Clever children, meaning the broad band of the ordinarily bright rather than the mad men of genius, can be fun to teach. School works for them. They are successful, they are generally keen and well behaved. It is not good either for staff relations or for other children if they are grouped together and taught always by the heads of departments. It is very probably also bad for the clever in social terms to be so favoured.

With the arrival of the common school, the clever, once separated off into enclaves where all were relatively bright, have become a minority. Whether this breeds in them understanding, familiarity and friendship, and breaks down social divisions, or whether it inculcates arrogance and self-satisfaction depends a great deal on how schools cope in general. If the organization of the school is such that the bright are in a clearly defined ghetto upon which the lion's share of attention is lavished, if the rights of the minority are implicitly preferred to those of the majority, then social tension is more likely to result.

In many schools, the chosen solution to this problem is not to separate children into clearly identified ability groups but to teach them all together in so-called mixed ability classes for at least the first year or two. In others, children are grouped by ability at least for some subjects while the job of teaching them is shared out among all the staff. At first sight it seems nonsense not to give the brightest classes to the brightest teachers, but the resentment caused by doing so can be great. It is widely considered essential for the morale of children and staff that all groups receive the same amount of attention from the brightest teachers, and the policy may go further. In schools which do not have mixed ability classes, there is a great temptation to give the least competent teachers – those least competent anyway in terms of class control and charisma – the best motivated classes. A student or probationary teacher will get an easier ride in such a class. Not all heads have the omnipresent spectre of wrathful fee-paying parents so clearly in mind as has the head of School E, who makes very sure that no boy is confronted by more than one student in a year and never in exam years. Students can, he reckons, cost pupils at least one grade at O-level.

Mixed ability teaching is perhaps the most hotly disputed feature of comprehensive schools. The logic behind it is impeccable. If selection into separate schools at eleven is premature, breeds self-fulfilling prophecies and high rates of failure, selection into separate streams in a common school must surely do the same.

Research work on under-achievement and early leaving in grammar schools, and on the effects of teachers' expectation upon children's performance, as reported in R. R. Dale and S. Griffith, *Down Stream – Failure in the Grammar School* (1975), provided the most respectable academic under-pinning. Dividing children up and declaring some clever or some stupid clearly jeopardizes the chances of the slower. Evidence of wasted talent in the C streams of grammar schools piled up in academic research. Government reports (*Early Leaving* in 1954, and the Newsom Report, *Half Our Future* in 1963), had articulated national concern at the losses.

Rather less definitive but still eminently respectable research also suggests that, while the slower lose by being labelled, the bright who are working well do not lose by the postponement of that labelling. The academic basis for this comes from work which shows that low achievement in children is associated with a vicious circle of bad performance, producing low expectations from outsiders, less demands made and less self-confidence instilled. It is the circle itself which is hard to break. Where the circle is virtuous – good work, high praise, high self-regard – it is equally resilient, Carl Braun suggested in an article in *Review of Educational Research* (spring 1976, vol. 46, no. 2).

From this arises the practice of suppressing records of children's achievement in their previous school. It is very common for ordinary subject teachers in secondary schools to be given first-year mixed ability classes with no indication at all of the previous standard reached by the children.

'Our aim here is to give them all a fresh start. No one comes into this school labelled with a label from their previous school.'

To find this principle asserted with such passion as here by the head of the first year in School G, which takes children at thirteen, is relatively unusual. It is very common in schools with transfer at eleven. And it means that children who have made a good start are returned to square one along with those who have not.

There is a simple reason for putting all new entrants in together to begin with. Secondary schools draw from a number of feeder schools, sometimes, in urban areas, from over a hundred. The styles, the standards and the curricula of these schools vary. Those who have been badly taught need a fair chance to catch up with those who have been well taught, and the secondary school will want to ensure a common base of knowledge in all its intake as the foundation for further work.

But mixed ability teaching is, in many schools, far more than a useful device for sorting out the new entrants, or a way of counteracting bad teaching and diverse curricula in feeder schools. It is a device adopted specifically to avoid labelling the stupid and to prevent the creation of slum classes which everyone dreads teaching. 'We don't want all the rotten apples in one basket.' It is hoped that the presence of the bright will raise the sights of the dim. And it is argued that there is in fact no such thing as a homogeneous class in even the most finely streamed school; that children should be encouraged to work at their own pace and that mixed ability organization, by making class teaching impossible, encourages this.

Teachers who favour mixed ability teaching sometimes have strong philosophical views on the subject. They maintain that all children are different; that all must be given an equal chance; that hierarchies of talent and rigid pecking orders are unacceptable; that competition is beneficial only to the winner; that, freed from cramping expectations, the apparently slow can do remarkable work and show talents which the traditional lectures, notes and written work style of academic teaching do not tap. 'It is not the ones who are best on paper who produce the most perceptive questions in class,' said a teacher of religious studies after taking a mixed ability class on the Pharisee and the publican.

In practice, mixed ability teaching does not work so well. For certain children, though not perhaps all that many, tough academic work is a pleasure and a challenge. For very many more it is a mystery and a bore. While some children, who may or may not be the academic ones, make craft-work a life's commitment, others – clever or dumb – regularly hammer their thumbs. What tends to happen is that classes of children taught in the same group for most of their subjects are fed the same diet: English, maths, languages, crafts and so forth. In the interests of equal opportunities, secondary schools begin each new subject from scratch, assuming nothing. The result can be as boring in craft subjects as in languages to competent children who have already made a good start in a subject. Home economics classes begin with, 'Now to boil an egg you ...' English classes may be confined for terms to books which bright children read in primary school. Maths may plod unendurably through the basics, 'to bring them all up to an acceptable minimum standard'.

Beyond a very limited diagnostic period, the boredom of such things is intolerable. Holding children back – 'because all can't none shall' – is an unwarranted oppression. Yet if classes are rigidly divided into ability groups and proceed at different rates and even follow different courses, it is a cruel confidence trick to pretend that it is possible for the diligent to catch up.

Her Majesty's Inspectorate's study of mixed ability teaching, published in 1978, made sorry reading. In many schools, the inspectors found boring courses, scruffy and inadequate materials, under-extended children and lack of academic content. Most classes were taught as a group, slowing to the pace of the average children within them. Where cleverer children were given extra work, it was often dull and repetitive.

At the same time, the report contained some evidence that the slower children were enjoying school and school work to an extent which surprised the inspectors. Courtesy, self-confidence and friendliness were marked. It seemed that while academic pace was getting lost, social attitudes were improving. Unfortunately, the inspectors failed to explore the dilemma they revealed: if the slower children gain by putting a brake on the clever ones in this way, whose interests are to be preferred?

A lead in sorting out the dilemma is clearly needed. In 1974, only one secondary school in ten surveyed by the National Child Development Study used mixed ability teaching in the first two years. Two years later, when Her Majesty's Inspectorate carried out their own survey, a quarter did so. Even allowing for the use of different questions and criteria, this means that mixed ability teaching is becoming far more common. It is therefore becoming ever more important to see that it works properly for all involved.

Advice is plentiful. In a document, 'Mixed Ability Grouping in Secondary Schools', drawn up ostensibly as guidance for teachers planning to introduce mixed ability teaching, Hampshire Education Authority accept much of the philosophical case against traditional teaching to streamed classes.

The relative dullness of work in academic groups (albeit of high quality in some areas) might be partly traceable to the fact that only a limited range of talents is given value ... Illustration in graphic forms, exploration of ideas through drama and role-play, imaginative leaping forward to new, untried ideas; these forms of attack on 'academic' subject areas are relatively under-valued or may be definitely discouraged.

But the handbook goes on to warn of the practical difficulties. In languages, it simply writes off the idea.

Mixed ability classes soon produce widely different levels of attainment and, with the oral and teacher-centred nature of much of the work, either less able pupils fall behind, or more able pupils increasingly mark time to allow others to catch up.

In other subjects it sets out the requirements, including meticulous planning and suitable materials.

... ensure that there are sufficient activities to occupy the fastest children all the time, but also that the slowest ones do those things that are most appropriate for their individual needs. Furthermore this must happen even when the teacher, who can only be in one place at a time, is not immediately available to provide guidance and support ... A major concern is the amount of time required for the production of structured materials ... A further factor is the level of expertise required by those producing materials of this kind.

A well-indexed collection of resource materials, films, books, slides, cassettes as well as the basic scheme of work are specified as essential, along with an efficient monitoring and assessment scheme. The document amounts to major discouragement of any mixed ability teaching which is not a radical change in the whole way teachers impart knowledge and inculcate skill. And it warns that such a radical change is expensive in terms of time, energy and money.

It is rare to go into mixed ability classes in schools where such a radical reorientation has taken place.

What we saw [said HMI in a report, *Gifted Children in Comprehensive Schools* (1977)] was mixed ability groups taught by whole class methods. While we found instances of mixed ability grouping, we had greater difficulty in finding mixed ability teaching ... Attempts at accommodating extremes of ability by using worksheets in the major disciplines were often unimpressive ... Gifted children merely finished faster than their fellows ... There is a risk that the very able may have a smaller share of teacher time than the less able.

But, the inspectors went on:

We observed that where gifted children were identified, the work of such children was often directed in a highly skilled and appropriate manner, despite limited time for dialogue with teachers, the two preconditions for such provision being the competence of the teacher to handle mixed ability groups and his/her insight and qualification in the area being taught.

In that study, the inspectors were concerned with the top 2 per cent of pupils, those who might score 130 or more on an IQ test or who showed a consistent high performance over the years – a much smaller group than those with whom this book is concerned. But the principles of identification and appropriate provision apply to all children, whatever form of grouping a school uses.

The way in which mixed ability teaching can go wrong when enthusiasm ebbs is well illustrated by School H, a city comprehensive taking 1,800 boys and girls from eleven to eighteen. Here the head had reluctantly come to the conclusion that mixed ability teaching was no longer working, though he had been one of the most enthusiastic pioneers of the idea twenty years ago.

The school withdrew the bottom two classes from the normal timetable and taught them separately. It then taught the rest in mixed ability classes for the first two years, with a second language offered to those who wanted it – and could cope with it – in the second year. This is a common enough pattern now, but it was not when this school introduced it. The practice was first adopted in the school, along with Nuffield maths and science, because of two things. First the head found when he experimented that he could get further through the syllabus with mixed classes taught by the methods which mixed ability makes necessary – namely, children working at their own pace – than he could with the top streamed groups alone. Secondly, when the children were divided into sets in the third year, the bright ones learnt much faster, with more grasp of the concepts and more enthusiasm than third-year bright pupils had shown before. Mixed ability in the third year never worked in his experience.

'By Christmas we had to revert to the other system. The bright were not being pushed and the others were falling too far behind. Mixed ability above the second years is just not on. It requires *very* exceptional teachers.'

What in retrospect seemed to him to have gone wrong was that some departments, particularly science, left to sort out their own groups, had extended mixed ability for too long and were teaching mixed O-level and CSE groups together in the fourth and fifth years instead of splitting them up. And, secondly, that there was a more fundamental flaw:

'It is essential that you have teachers who really know what standards they are going for at various levels.'

When he started mixed ability classes, all the staff in the school had taught streamed or setted groups and knew what could be done by and expected from the cleverest and the stupidest. Twenty years later, most of his teachers had never taught homogeneous groups of twelve-year-olds.

'If they are to set the standard high enough and not hold back and bore the brightest, they must have had experience of teaching academic children. If they are not to destroy the morale of the slowest, they must know the techniques for helping them.'

He was almost tempted to think a twenty-year cycle was needed so that mixed ability teaching could be practised by those who had experienced the range and variation of selected classes while setted classes were taught by those aware of the surprises which can come from avoiding preconceived notions of what is possible from particular children.

Where mixed ability teaching is done well, the most noticeable thing about it is often the extraordinary dedication of the teachers. Indeed, the same can be said of comprehensive schools in general however they are organised. The head of one highly successful school which did no mixed ability teaching above the first year said, 'Very few indeed of my staff work less than an eleven-hour day, and a lot do much more than that ... It is extremely exhausting.'

The head of a successful English department in School J, teaching mixed ability classes right up to the fifth year, described the work involved as 'crucifying'. In the summer they had to mark and cross-mark project work for O-level and CSE exams for 280 girls. It took all nine teachers in the department – since all shared the fifth-year teaching – at least two weeks, working until 10 p.m. every night. It was only by designing their own CSE exams to fit in with one of the O-level boards' project-based English exams that they were able to make the mixed ability system work. This involved writing large parts of the course themselves. On top of this, he found that, as the school tightened its assessment and monitoring procedures, the number of meetings was rising, adding to the calls on his time and taking him away from his teaching.

Not all schools can rely on finding this sort of dedication in their teachers. None could expect to find it in all of them. Even so, a study of secondary school teachers' working days published in 1978 by the National Foundation for Educational Research showed that the average secondary teacher worked the equivalent of a forty-hour week forty-eight weeks a year. Only a fifth of this time was spent actually teaching; the rest was spent in preparation, duplicating, marking, talking to parents, advising children, supervising, reading, clerical chores, discipline and coping with emergencies.

The administration of today's schools can be horrendous, and is sometimes irritatingly trivial. One head whom I visited had just come from checking that someone else had checked that the school minibus's first-aid kit conformed to EEC regulations. And good administration is vital to the efficient running of large schools.

It can very well be argued that work of this kind is nothing more than society might expect of full-salaried professional people, particularly when the hours are so distributed as to provide some twelve or thirteen weeks' holiday a year. The trouble is that, like all averages, this conceals immense variations. While some work a ten- or twelve-hour day, the actual timetable obligation of an ordinary teacher is probably around twenty hours a week (thirty-five out of a total of a possible forty thirty-five-minute periods in a week – a fairly heavy teaching load). This variation could well be increased if the campaign launched in the spring of 1978 by one of the major teachers' unions, the National Association of Schoolmasters/Union of Women Teachers (NAS/UWT) gathers pace. The union is claiming, though it has no legal grounds for doing so, that all activities by teachers outside the normal timetable are voluntary. While they protest that, of course, their members do and will continue to work the sort of week the NFER survey showed to be the average (the survey is used as grist to the campaign), they are resisting the idea that it is part of their contract that they be expected to do so. Some would go so far along this line as to maintain that marking books, preparing lessons and attending staff meetings after 4 p.m. are all voluntary commitments. Uncertainty about the amount of work a school can expect from its own staff does not make its task easier.

If mixed ability teaching is often bad and clearly worries the parents of clever children, it must be said that such evidence as there is suggests a remarkable resilience in those children. There is nothing concrete to show, despite public belief to the contrary, that a couple of years of going slowly in academic subjects harms children's academic achievements a few years later. The National Child Development Study, in a survey which covered 6,000 sixteen-year-olds, found no evidence that mixed ability grouping in the first two years of secondary school affected any children's performance at sixteen when compared with that of children taught in streamed classes. And there was some evidence that mixed ability classes gave the slower a better chance of taking public exams.

A much smaller-scale study, which compared the effects of mixed ability teaching and streaming in the first year of secondary school, was carried out at Banbury School in Oxfordshire. This showed no bad effects for the able and some slight gains for others both during the mixed ability year and later. The follow-up study at sixteen found that, even after the children were streamed, differences persisted. There was some evidence that the exam results of the middle ability children from the mixed ability classes were a little better. There was no evidence that those of the brightest were any worse.

This study also produced one joker. It indicated clearly a tendency for unstreamed pupils to opt for science when they made their subject choices in the fourth year and for streamed pupils to opt for languages. The difference was particularly marked among middle ability girls and the pattern carried on residually when they chose subjects in the sixth form.

Bias to science in state schools compared with independent schools and the plight of languages generally will be discussed later (pages 95–100) in the context of national patterns. The light thrown on these two linked topics by the Banbury study is all the more illuminating for having been totally unexpected. It must at once be said that not all schools enjoy Banbury's clear distinctions. Some scarcely seem to know whether they have mixed ability teaching or not, let alone to have any way of monitoring the results. If timetables are arranged, as they often are, so that children in one year do, say, maths at the same time, the maths department staff can, and often do, have the freedom to decide how to split the children up.

But there will not be enough teachers to teach a whole year together in most subjects, including languages. In School G, which was strongly committed to ensuring that all children had the same chances and did not stream at all, the staff had some flexibility. The pupils were divided into years (about 300 in each), and each year, for the purpose of timetabling, into two halves roughly equal in ability. Each faculty – world studies, maths, science, languages, English and so on – got half a year together (about 150 children) and could group them how they liked. There were no options between faculties, but within them the staff could decide what courses to put on – history, geography, physics, rural science and so forth – as well as who would do them. The maths department set by ability after half a term. The science department did not do so until the beginning of the second year, by which time the children were fourteen. Then exam courses were chosen which in fact acted as a form of streaming, science technology leading only to CSE, the doube option integrated science course to two O-levels.

The head of the language department, like many language teachers, disliked mixed ability teaching and set as much as possible. But because he only had half the year at a time, he could not put the thirty best linguists together and push them on for O-level. He regularly ended up with two classes in which half were doing O-level and half CSE French. He reckoned that it costs the bright ones grades at O-level. They rarely get A grades. And the bright pupils said that their French lessons were intolerably boring. They laughed bitterly and described it as 'like going on a great long hike'. They also did very badly. In mock exams in 1978, the top sets averaged 40 per cent with a range of marks from 67 per cent to 6 per cent. And this in a school where only the top half of the pupils did French after fourteen.

The fault here probably lay partly with the break at thirteen which is widely acknowledged to make reasonable attainment in languages very difficult to achieve. But the school's organization was not helping. For philosophical reasons, it was forcing on reluctant teachers broader ability teaching groups than were strictly necessary.

The wide range of ability in many comprehensive school classes is, as I have said, among the things which most bothers the parents of clever children.

Wide ability classes are virtually inevitable in small comprehensives. Take, for example, School K, a school of 700 girls in a city in the midlands. Over half the girls came in at eleven with a reading age of under nine. Four out of five were from immigrant families. Though there were some clever students, there were not enough to produce reasonable-sized classes for both O-level and CSE in the fourth and fifth years, even with options limited to choosing two from history, general science, biology and chemistry, with either physics, or needlework, French or religious studies. This school therefore did not offer O-level except in the sixth form, and the clever girls were taught in classes with a wide range of ability where the level of their work depended entirely on the skill of the teacher.

The level of work in some of the classes seemed pretty unexciting. One was a fourth-year geography class where twenty-five girls were studying the formation of river valleys. The teacher gave a lecture from the front, then a tape/slide presentation, then set two questions from last year's CSE paper on the subject for homework. The teacher went through the questions in some detail before letting the class go. Any reasonably quick child would have finished that homework before the bell went.

In another class it was better. A fifth-year maths class was studying for CSE: thirty-one in the class. They rattled through a lesson on probability, starting with a pack of cards and ending up with all the proper notation and formulas without apparently losing anyone on the way. Half the class would, the teacher reckoned, get grade 1.

This school seemed deliberately to sacrifice the more able up to sixteen. It then tried to compensate them later. Half the girls stay on in the sixth form, and the timetable was extended to 5 p.m., though the school day officially ended at 3.30. The extra time was used for sixth-form O- and A-level teaching, and a number of girls did O-level in their first sixth-form year, and then a two-year A-level course.

Such compensation does not really go far. Even with this sort of special arrangement, the school could offer only six academic A-level subjects, though it also achieved impressive A-level work in practical subjects.

This particular school raised some important issues for comprehensives. First, many of its pupils were from Asian families. They got off to a slow start academically because they first had to learn English. For these girls the three-year sixth-form course could be invaluable, the difference between success or failure in their adopted country. But as a general pattern, for bright children not so handicapped at an earlier stage, it would represent a waste of time and a waste of public money.

Secondly, there cannot be any confidence that all the schools which do only CSE in the fifth year provide this sort of compensation in the sixth form, nor that all those who could have done O-level will stay on.

Thirdly, negotiating an extended day can be a tricky business. The head of this particular school had been there many years. She had considerable charisma and a remarkably clear picture of the sort of commitment she expected from the teachers who were taken on. 'I'm a bit of a martinet really. I like people to work like stink right up to the bell and I expect them to run clubs and things like that.' Many heads would envy her the school's cohesive and dedicated staff.

Fourthly, six academic A-level subjects are generally regarded as too few to chose from. In the national league table of most-popular A-level subjects, there are now nine in which over 20,000 pupils pass each year. Ten years ago there were only five: maths (all kinds lumped together), English, physics, history and chemistry, in that order. But economics and geography broke the 20,000 barrier in 1969, biology in 1973 and general studies in 1976. These top nine include no modern languages and no craft subjects. (French lies tenth.)

Limitations of this kind have fuelled the anti-comprehensive campaign. In the *Black Paper 1977*, the fourth in a series of polemics against comprehensives produced by a group of conservative education pundits since 1969, Robert Vigars, leader of the Conservative opposition on the Inner London Education Authority, wrote an article pointing out how patchy sixth-form provision was in London comprehensives. His article blithely ignored the continuing presence of some forty grammar schools in London at that time, and it concentrated to a considerable extent on craft subjects, which are, after sixteen, probably better and more frequently taught in further education colleges. But, for all that the point is a telling one: if schools are going to be called comprehensive they must make available to their bright pupils a reasonable spread of subject choices after sixteen. At present many fail to do so.

In 1978, Dudley Fiske, Chief Education Officer for Manchester, as reported in the *Observer* for 5 November 1978, produced some evidence of an anecdotal kind on the effects of school size for a meeting of the Secondary Heads Association. A-level results in Manchester schools have been causing worry for some time. Sixth-form work is spread among twenty-six high schools in the city, and, as a result, some teaching groups are extremely small. Dudley Fiske's preliminary inquiries showed that the smaller schools with small sixth-form groups tended to produce worse A-level results.

Eric Briault, who became a professor at Sussex University when he retired as Inner London's education officer, has been carrying out more systematic research on the effects of falling school rolls. He has been trying in particular to establish whether there is a size below which secondary schools should not be allowed to fall if they are to work well. By 1979, the study was beginning to produce tentative results, namely, that in schools below about 900 it becomes extremely expensive to preserve adequate sixth-form work. Staffing sixth-form courses drains staff and money from the lower school, producing larger classes and less money for books. In larger schools, on the other hand, the opposite appeared to be true: the existence of a sixth form benefits the lower school by bringing in extra teachers, extra money and extra stimulation. (This study is to be published in 1980.)

Small comprehensives have been accepted as a result of popular demand. In some places, of which London is the best-known example, this was done because only by preserving the identity of certain popular grammar schools could consent be gained for turning them into comprehensives. There is much protestation that such schools can work provided they restrict severely the number of choices which they offer so that those with high ability can be taught together most of the time. It is often pointed out that much larger schools, like School G, do not make use of their size to produce homogeneous teaching groups.

Some large schools provide a very wide range of options which spread the bright out in their fourth and fifth years. Some make it a matter of principle to do so, offering children the opportunity to study what they most enjoy. One school I visited offers as many as forty-three options at fourteen, another twenty-six. The net result is that, in many schools, O-level and CSE candidates are taught together. Decisions as to which child does which exam are then put off until perhaps a term or two before the exam.

The evidence that is beginning to emerge suggests that it may only be comprehensives with over 1,000 pupils and with a limited range of options which can really provide classes of reasonable pace for the top 20 per cent of the ability range. Sixth-form work is the most obvious casualty, but O-level work may well suffer too.

Comprehensives are living with an unresolved, and possibly unresolvable, conflict between egalitarianism and élitism. It is a conflict which is likely to divide members of staff as much as it divides outsiders. It is not therefore surprising that head teachers seem so often to duck the issue, leaving individual department heads to work out their own policies.

Unfortunately, such abdication produces serious weakness. In a pamphlet, *Ten Good Schools* (1977), Her Majesty's Inspectorate identified a clear philosophy as one of the main characteristics of a good school and the leadership of the head as one of the most important factors in producing such clarity. The way children are divided into groups inside a school is an indication of that school's underlying philosophy; it is not the only one, but a very important one.

The uncompromising nature of School D's organization is rare. Thirteen-year-olds were divided as soon as they arrived into twelve forms ranked by ability. The top four forms were launched on a set O-level course of maths, English and five other subjects of their choice. The next two forms did a mixed CSE and O-level course, with no choices except between woodwork, art and domestic science. The next four were on a CSE course of English, maths, geography and general science, with either history or economics, art, music or religious education. The last two forms did maths, English, science, geography and history with some practical subjects. These bottom two forms were not expected to get many exam passes, if any. The exam results for the school as a whole were good. But there were social snags. Pupils in the top ability groups had been heard to refer to the lower groups, in which the immigrant intake was concentrated, as 'the barbarian hordes', and one of the teachers explained to me how hopeless some of the low-band children were by describing the trouble he had had in getting across the idea of housing density.

'I drew out all these little plots and put six houses in one and twenty in the other. Then I asked which had the greater density.' There had been a long silence, and then the girl he was talking to said she didn't know. 'It depends,' she said, 'how many families live in each house.' 'You see,' he said, 'it's almost impossible to teach them.'

A school with a very different but equally uncompromising policy is the new community school at Sutton-in-Ashfield in Nottinghamshire. It, too, ran into snags, and ones of a more public kind. The radical nature of the school's policy and curriculum invalidated comparisons with the 'all face the front and listen to me' style of learning which flourished in School D. It also provoked great anxiety among many of those unfamiliar with new ideas in education, and in particular among people who had themselves done well under the conventional system and who had children who also did well in traditional classrooms. Among other things, the school carried its convictions to the point of offering no O-levels in the fifth year.

When the county council swung to the Conservatives in 1977, the grumblings of some parents, ostensibly over the specific case of a class discussion of swearing, were taken up by the council, who proposed to investigate the school. The teachers protested. Her Majesty's Inspectors were called in. The ensuing report, completed in 1978, commended the school as 'a notable experiment in education', and found 'much work of creditable quality particularly in literature, mathematics and science', an excellent record system, and pupils who generally behaved well and liked their school and their work. The only substantial criticism: the staff were working too hard. To reduce the sizes of mixed ability groups, they had given up almost all of their free periods.

It is hardly surprising that such clear-cut examples are not general. Comprehensives are on the defensive, the job is new and difficult, the teachers very ordinary mortals. It is much easier to find woolliness and a botched job, to find children who have had a remarkably boring time and who reckon that they get away with murder. 'As long as you do some home-work, no one really bothers much what it's like. It's good if it's handed in on time.' 'I really wish I'd been made to work harder when I first came here.'

Burnt-out cases, children who will never again do as good work as they did before the age of thirteen, are unheard of in comprehensives. Lazy and bored children, children who have spent most of a year repeating work they have done before at another school, are not; nor are those who, to keep in with their friends, take pains not to become the appointed 'brains' of the class, teacher's pet.

'I used to behave badly on purpose in order to get into the class's good books by being anti-teacher. You see there was quite a lot of bullying about working hard.' This sixth-form girl has seen her school, School J, change for the better since then, but such stories are common. Sometimes, if the atmosphere is amiable it seems not to matter. 'Yes, you get called a swot, but you get used to that and they soon stop if they want some help with something' – so said a remarkably relaxed and cheerful sixth-former in another school, School L, a boy whose passion was designing and building model planes.

A girl in School L welcomed the relaxed attitude. 'A friend I was at school with until I was eleven got a scholarship to one of those very high-powered schools. I got one too but we moved house. He's doing A-levels a year earlier than me and he's absolutely fed up and turned off the whole thing. I wouldn't want that sort of pressure.' But then School L was another example of an impressively hard-working, cohesive, success-orientated school, trying to satisfy a lot of ambitious, middle-class parents on the rich outskirts of a major city.

It was one of its local authority's show schools. According to one of their senior advisors, in many other less glamorous schools in the city only extremely low-level work was being done. An ordinarily bright child would, in his view, have little chance in those schools of going on to higher education.

To sum up, the factors which have made the work of the comprehensives peculiarly difficult are constant organizational change over recent years, both in schools and in local authorities; enormous pressure as the common school brings under one roof all the conflicting demands, the different habits, attitudes, values and expectations of a multifarious society; crushing work for teachers, many of them never trained in the skills they now need if they are to develop the talents of all children, instead of just some; public parsimony in the resources made available to do the job. It amounts to more than enough to explain why the comprehensives have not done better. Indeed, it is all the more remarkable that there should be no objective evidence of deterioration, even on the narrow academic front.

What there has been is an erosion of differentials for the sort of families who can assume with confidence that their children would have been on the privileged end of the old selection procedures, or who could once have bought their way out of failure, but can now no longer afford to do so; an erosion of differentials in the sense that these children no longer win through at eleven to a relatively privileged and tranquil world apart, where they would have been machined for entry to the middle and upper occupational ranks of society. Erosion of differentials ever causes bitterness, even if the higher placed have lost only in relative not in real terms. Closing the gap, postponing distribution of life chances, is a threat to those who are successful early. And it is not surprising that people are anxious and angry.

The clever are now asked to wait longer for the differentiation which will lift them on to further learning in order that none who might advance with them are left behind. They are asked to do so partly on altruistic grounds. By so waiting, they can help the achievement and the self-respect of those who will not have much chance for further study. The clever may gain by this delay, if in the process they grow up more familiar and at ease with people of all capacities than the leaders of the nation's enterprises have done in the past. They may gain, too, if the time is used to try out a wider range of subjects and skills than is possible when academic pressure is tougher.

That much being said, other questions remain. How long is it practicable or wise not to make distinctions? What can be done at all stages to ensure that talent is not lost, that children are not unnecessarily bored and that the nation is not deprived of serious, competent and well-trained young people?

The answer is partly a matter of public policy, of deciding which are the important values to be fostered, what talents, competencies and attitudes are the ones desired. It is partly a matter of balancing desirable aims against available resources, both human and financial.

As part of this process, it is important to be clear about what can be done in comprehensive schools which have succeeded in overcoming the chaos and muddle of the early years. The next chapter describes how such schools, required to cope with the conflicts and pressures described in this chapter, may be forging something which is rather different from conventional academic education.

In opening up chances to those who did not have them before, radical changes have been made in the way children are taught. These changes aim to give new status to skills and characteristics previously undervalued. They have not always been successful and it is therefore tempting to denigrate the underlying idea. This may be a mistake.

Some of the work (which I take to be the best) that I have been shown in comprehensives has been so entirely different from *all* of the work I have been shown in grammar and independent schools as to give pause for thought. The main difference was that the best of the comprehensive work came over as more interesting.

Teachers in comprehensives say it again and again, doing themselves no service by wrapping the point up in a mass of jargon about 'insights drawn from the real life experience of the child'. The jargon about 'relevance' infuriates anyone who believes that one of the pleasures of education is the chance to learn abstruse things of no obvious relevance to everyday life. It is also infuriating to see endless hours wasted metaphorically rediscovering the wheel when a brief lesson from a teacher would get a pupil further faster. None the less, where rigorous standards are insisted upon and this is combined with a heuristic approach to learning, there is something beguiling about the freshness of the results. Also, the tasks performed bear a closer relation to tasks met in everyday life than does some academic school work.

The sort of difference I mean, though the example is not one of excellence in either case, is well if crudely illustrated by two sets of homework given to thirteen-year-olds in one week. One class at a highly academic independent day school were given a chapter of a history textbook to read. They had to make notes and be ready for a test the following week. The chapter covered the end of the Middle Ages and dealt in particular with the invention of printing.

The other class, at a comprehensive, was also studying the end of the Middle Ages and was simply told, 'Find out what you can about Caxton and write a page and a half.' The task meant a trip to the library for any child whose home did not contain the necessary reference books, an impossible requirement for many. Yet this, unlike the other assignment, contained the challenge of research. The other concentrated on the hard slog of disciplined work.

As able children educated in comprehensives right through their school days begin to come through to public exams and to university entrance in growing numbers, it should be possible to see not only whether there is any clear change in standards judged by existing measures, but also whether there are other differences between able young people brought up in inclusive or exclusive schools; whether there is a different quality to the way they work; whether a different type of child succeeds; whether there is more self-reliance and less spoonfeeding.

There are in the national figures indications that science flourishes in state schools. There are indications that in all schools, but more in comprehensives, languages are suffering. There are indications that clever young people in comprehensives are not attracted to the ancient universities, and perhaps not to any universities. There are signs of a growing preference for work rather than academic higher education. All these trends are considered in later chapters.

First, however, I want to describe in the most anecdotal terms the sort of differences I have seen between good selective and good comprehensive education, hoping in the process to cast some light on what exactly it is that parents get if they pay for exclusive schooling. (For, increasingly, exclusive schooling is being confined to the fee-paying sector.)

To embark on comparisons between selective and non-selective schools is a dangerous business. To embark on comparisons between selective independent schools and non-selective local authority maintained ones is even more fool-hardy. Yet this is the comparison parents are making all the time. Increasingly it has been the only one they could make, since free selective education has been vanishing.

Few perhaps are rich enough to have the choice. C. Howard, a firm of insurance brokers specializing in school fee schemes, say that four out of five families using their policies are having to make economies to meet private fees. Many more people probably wish they had the option. Are they right in thinking that what they would get would be better? The head of School C, which is a country town middle school, amuses himself by working out what it would cost people to send their children to his well-appointed, purpose-built school with its excellent art and music, if it was a private school. 'It would cost them a great deal – and then they wouldn't get what they get now because they'd lose the social mix and sense of community.'

It is becoming increasingly difficult, however, to make any judgement in terms of quality. There are good schools and bad schools in both sectors. And over and above that, there are some things the two have to offer which are intrinsically different. What you get from a good comprehensive is not the same as what you get from a good selective school.

For a start, the atmosphere is different. Sixteen children in every twenty leaving a state school go straight to work, if they can get it. Only one goes on to a degree course. By contrast, little more than one in three leaving an ex-direct grant school (most of them now independent) goes to work, while nearly two out of three go to some sort of further course, half of them to degree courses.

Comprehensives cannot in equity concentrate on university entry as their main priority. They certainly cannot justify putting much emphasis on entry to Oxford and Cambridge. They are obliged to present to their pupils a very wide range of possibilities after school. They cannot afford to subscribe to the view that high academic standards are 'best'.

By contrast, a major public school, School M, which sends

49

in any year about 50 out of 140 sixth-formers to Oxford and Cambridge and almost all the rest to other universities, can afford to concentrate on academic achievement and has little incentive to do anything else. Practical and applied subjects are relegated to spare time. The school turns out virtually no one with their eye on a career in design, production or industrial management.

For an individual child who is clever but who prefers practical to academic pursuits, this can be seriously cramping. On a wider front, it produces a distortion in the preparation for working life of a substantial number of clever young people. In such a school, a child will not have a good chance of carving out for himself a non-academic career of a kind which will be regarded by his peers, his teachers or his parents as a success.

In a class of sixth-formers in School M, all expected to go to university. Would any ultimately expect to work in industry? None. Would any consider going to a polytechnic? Pause. Then, 'I did share a study with someone last year who wanted to opt out and go to North London Poly. His parents were appalled at first but now they're really being awfully good about it.'

Did they mind that public exams in art can only be done in spare time and that there are no other practical subjects on the timetable at all? 'They couldn't really put art on the timetable. There's not time and it's really not any use. You can't go up to Oxford saying I've got an A in art, can you? And you have to have Latin for some things. I mean there's really nothing the school can do about it. It all depends on the university. After all, that's what this school is for, to get people into university.'

School M takes day pupils and boarders, mainly boys with girls in the sixth form. It is one of the most sought-after public schools because many parents see it as the key to Oxford and Cambridge university places. This is so much the case that there have been irate parents demanding their fees back when the school refused to allow a child to take the entrance exams on the grounds that they were not good enough.

Such schools complain loudly about parents' excessive ambition and anxiety. But access to high status in our society is coming increasingly to depend on educational qualifications. Reverence for academic laurels as opposed to practical skills has become deep seated in British society in the last hundred years. It is reinforced by the manifest material advantage accruing to those who do have academic qualifications. Ambitious parents are, in the most pragmatic terms, right to want a solid, academic schooling and a good university place for their children.

Comprehensives, trying to establish their credentials in a hostile world, find themselves severely limited by the expectations of such parents when it comes to considering what they should do for clever children. Even so, because they must cater for all children whatever the temptation to stress academic excellence, they willy-nilly put a much wider range of possibilities before the bright. In many comprehensives, practical courses are, after the first couple of years mainly used to provide satisfying courses for the non-academic. Clever children may find they have little time in an academic timetable to take craft subjects. But the facilities are there under their noses, and so are the people who can teach these subjects and children who are good at them. They have the chance to use the facilities, and other career possibilities than academic ones are automatically presented to them.

A possible effect of this diversity is indicated by the high proportion of comprehensive pupils compared with pupils from selective schools who go to polytechnics. On the positive side, this may be because psychologically they are prepared to consider a wider range of courses than are pupils from selective schools. However widely practical and creative activities are made available as voluntary, extra-curricular activities in academic schools, they are thus automatically labelled by this relegation as being not serious. A child in one highly academic independent school said, 'We think of our art lessons as our gossip time.' In some independent schools, even prep schools with children from eight years old, there is a marked scarcity of such lessons even as recreation.

On the negative side, the lack of academic pressure may

mean that comprehensive children are going to polytechnics because they cannot get into universities. Children of equivalent or lesser intelligence who have been to more single-minded schools may be crowding them out. (The whole question of higher education places is discussed in more detail in Chapter 4.)

The narrowness of an academic curriculum is sometimes regretted by independent school teachers, yet they have little choice but to preserve it since this is the main selling point for their very expensive services. Competition for places in academic schools which are good at getting people into university reinforces this effect. It also means the narrowing is extended to younger children.

Ex-direct grant schools and girls' independent schools are able to draw direct from maintained primary schools. The main boys' public schools cannot do this since they usually do not take pupils before about thirteen. This means they have to depend on preparatory schools to do the foundation work for them. Competition for places at School M meant that boys were sent to private prep schools at eight.

One such school was School N. It fed half its pupils into School M at about thirteen. In 1978, nearly a hundred people applied for twenty places at School N. It had no gymnasium, no art room, no music room. Its pupils did 800 hours of Latin before the age of thirteen and had only one period of art a week (in their classroom) after the age of ten or eleven. By thirteen, many of them were up to O-level standard in English, maths and Latin. Their French was good, science poor. By fifteen the brightest will be in the sixth form at School M, devoting most of their time to studying three main subjects.

Public schools mutter about the prep school connection: 'We'd dearly love to open up the entry to a much wider group,' they say. They have even been known to turn down the force-fed products of particular prep schools as burnt out and useless though apparently good on the exams. But beyond this, they hesitate to change things. One of the best prep schools in the country recently protested to a major public school at the sophistication of their Latin scholarship papers

nd got the answer, 'Well, there are plenty of prep schools
ʋho will do it for us, so why shouldn't we ask for it?'

But there is a certain feeling of solidarity in the private
ector. 'We don't really want to upset the prep schools. They
lo send us some very good people.' The prep schools are under
evere pressure already as numbers fall, primary schools im-
ɔrove and schools leavened by the ex-direct grant schools,
ɡrow more liberal in their admission policies.

The education of a child brought up on this pattern con-
rasts sharply with that of a child attending first a state pri-
nary school and then a comprehensive. Such a child is very
ikely to follow a common course up to thirteen which will in-
ɔlude at least four periods a week of practical subjects: wood-
ʋork, metalwork, possibly some design and technical drawing,
ɔooking, needlework, art, possibly pottery. The diet varies
ʋith the school and the sex of the child. Unless he/she is
extraordinary and has been deliberately accelerated on an
ndividual basis, there is no chance of being anywhere near
Ɔ-level standard in anything by thirteen.

The comprehensives have a much better chance of turning
ɔut their clever people with a practical bias. And they may
lo so. In 1978, Oxfordshire County Council applied for eight
ɔrovisional patents to cover entries for the Alcan/Oxfordshire
schools design competition before putting them on display. At
the same time, the Independent Schools Careers Organization
ɔulletin for spring 1978 lamented the total lack of independent
school entrants for a design competition for schools sponsored
by the General Electric Company.

There are, of course, a number of independent and grammar
schools which are very good on the craft and design side. And
when they are good they are likely to be very good because of
having a selected entry. Many independent schools will get
better in this respect. The search for funds by independent
schools to pay for art and craft facilities is gathering pace. One
public school is campaigning to raise £300,000 for a design
technology block. Another has excellent facilities paid for by
a major industrial company.

But virtually all the comprehensive schools in the country

with children over eleven, middle schools and secondaries have art and craft facilities, and often on a scale the private sector would have a job to match. Such facilities, and the materials needed for such courses, are extremely expensive and the independent sector is anxious not to raise fees more than necessary.

The move into creative and applied subjects in the independent sector matches the growing concern in the state sector about high academic standards. Both movements tend to add more to the amount of work expected of school children. They are asked to do more things and still to do everything they did before just as well as they did it before. There are no signs yet of any national willingness to argue out the relative values of breadth and academic specialization in terms removed from active political battles about standards.

In a paper prepared for a conference on comprehensive schools in York in 1977, Her Majesty's Inspectorate (HMI) regretted the heavy academic emphasis after thirteen. 'Generally speaking, the more able pupils acquire a heavily loaded academic timetable, in which the aesthetic/creative side of their curriculum may suffer severely.'

The inspectors fail altogether to acknowledge the dilemma: already comprehensives, by setting children on a broad general course to thirteen or fourteen, are leaving things very late. These children are being given much less time to clear the academic exam hurdles than their rivals. This is suspected of lowering academic attainment, and some people in the universities believe the percentage of children from the maintained schools coming into higher education of all kinds will fall if nothing is done.

Yet, lightening the academic load, as HMI appear to want, could only make matters worse – if bad they be.

The inspectorate's own schizophrenia is the clearest example of the country's schizophrenia on this subject. The two things are not fundamentally compatible. If the inspectorate, who are not politically involved, could now take a lead in spelling out the choices which confront the schools, they would perform a very necessary national service. It would be even better if they were to be joined by powerful voices in the universities since they are regarded as the custodians of standards.

What the inspectorate have done so far, and it is in a sense part of the same exercise, is to provide some strongly voiced opinions on how the sharpness of the dichotomy can be minimized; how schools can, by good practice, lessen the disadvantages for the clever. As the series of pamphlets, *Matters for Discussion*, lengthens, this guidance will become clearer. The message is, however, obscured by failure to address the central questions: how to extend the faster children without depressing the rest and how to foster creativity without destroying academic work.

Clear consideration of these matters is bedevilled by the independent sector's vigorous salesmanship and the universities' preference for students formed in a comfortably familiar mould. It is also bedevilled by the enormous financial implications involved in accepting that, if education is to be both broader and of a constant or rising standard in individual specialisms, it is bound to take longer. These issues are discussed in more detail in Chapter 5. First, however, for some concrete examples of the different work in schools produced by different emphases.

School P was a new community school of 1,400 twelve- to eighteen-year-old boys and girls. The 300 entrants in each year were allocated to a foundation course staffed by ten tutors with remedial teachers and music and drama specialists to help them. Children's abilities were tested 'in a relaxed way' in the first term, and these initial assessments were supplemented by the opinions of the tutors who taught them for half the week.

The school had been specially designed with inter-connecting rooms round central halls or libraries so as to encourage and make possible team teaching with flexible groups of children. The same style of teaching was also used after the first year, though children then spent more time with specialist teams of teachers. Half a year's intake, 150 children, were time-tabled together for each major subject area, and six teachers were allocated to them. The teachers then decided how to divide the children up. This meant that the bright or the slow, for example, could be withdrawn at certain times for special help; a hundred could watch a television programme or attend a science demonstration while five teachers did some extra work with the remaining fifty; a dozen could rehearse three scenes from *Macbeth* while another dozen got help with reading. The school even had double science labs so that two classes could do science together. Experiments were not duplicated and the teachers could supplement one another's expertise – 'you watch each other, it's very good for teaching standards.'

Dividing children into fixed classes by ability had to be justified in this school even after the second year (that is, for children of fourteen or above). 'It might be appropriate across, say, three forms. We have tried it in languages but it may go away. The gains are not enough because it decreases the motivation of the less able and may exacerbate the problems of adolescence,' was the head's view.

Only in maths were children put into ability groups early on. Within the blocked timetable, the best mathematicians were brought together to take O-level a year early. They took further maths at the end of the fifth year. In other subjects, once exam courses began, differences inevitably developed between those doing physics, chemistry and biology O-levels and those doing a combined science course, 'science and man', designed by the school as a single CSE subject.

In order to make this system work, School P wrote 90 per cent of its own learning materials for the first year. There was a printer in the community centre who printed their materials for them to a standard which many schools would envy. The building was new. The staff had all been hired to work in such a system, and commitment to it had been a re-quirement. Because of the radical nature of the design – both of the school and the curriculum – it had never been short of well-qualified enthusiasts, many of whom worked a sixty-hour week, adding community work to school teaching. It had, in short, much going for it.

Academic results were not, however, good. The first fifth-year results (only one group of children had reached this age by 1978) showed an average of five passes per pupil, but these included passes down to grade 5 CSE, which is not distinguished. There were extenuating circumstances. Few pupils would have had a full secondary course in the school. New pupils of all ages came in all the time as new housing went up in the area. There are few clever children. All the same, the local authority inspectors were not satisfied with the level of tough academic work being done.

The head, by contrast, was not satisfied with that sort of judgement. 'It is a mistake which the new comprehensives made in the 1960s competing with the grammar schools on their own terms. We believe in encouraging. We push as hard as we can in a nice way. If you do it in a nasty way you may succeed but you can destroy. This is the 1970s and you've got to do things differently.'

A school like this raises impossible questions about how far it is right to give fourteen-year-olds so much control over how hard they work, over whether they opt for the toughest course they can manage. The head said the tendency was to opt up rather than down – 'this is encouraged provided they won't fail'.

There was no way of measuring, for children of any ability, the merits of some of the work this school did. For example, they put on a play based on the history of the area. It was researched and written by children and performed by them with teachers and local people, including some who took part in the original events.

In the same county there is a highly academic grammar school, School Q, which made a total contrast. It produced remarkable exam results and university entrance successes. Not all the defenders of academic values were as crass as one of their young English teachers, but his attitude did throw some light on the essential differences. 'Oh yes,' he said, 'we do a lot of plays in class with the younger ones, two or three a year. Mainly Shakespeare. There's not really anything much else – a lot of secondary modern stuff of course – but nothing that's really intellectually demanding.'

Education officials in the county, so sceptical of the academic results at School P, took the view that School Q went in for too much academic cramming and was getting boys into Oxford and Cambridge ahead of brighter but less well-coached candidates. When I visited School Q, they were bending every nerve to discourage one boy from becoming a cabinet maker. 'He's much too bright. He'll be bored and regret it. He ought at least to do a timber technology degree before he decides.'

The school had recently started to run public speaking competitions between its houses because they found their older pupils, while excellent on paper, were rather tongue tied. No doubt they were also piqued by the consistent victories of School F, which is their neighbouring secondary modern school. School F regularly won the local Rotary Club's annual public speaking competition. Their success was largely due, the head said, to an excellent drama department.

The anti-academic view can, of course, be taken too far. Everyone would sympathise with the familiar lamentations of two English teachers in a sixth-form college, School R, over the standard of spelling and punctuation among children coming to them from local schools. But should their other equally loudly voiced complaint, that 'too much emphasis is being placed on creative writing as opposed to creative reaction to a great text', be taken equally seriously? These teachers minded passionately that many of the young people who have passed O-levels have 'plenty of ability and enthusiasm but no critical training at all'. They found that independent school pupils (a quarter of the college's intake is from independent schools) had come across subjects, 'as academic disciplines instead of all this child-centred learning'; while a lot of the state school pupils 'have not come across reading as a discipline at all'. Even the comprehensive school pupils' enthusiasm, something new in these teachers' experience, was regarded as a mixed blessing. 'I think it mainly comes from having had too easy a ride ... They have scarcely studied Shakespeare, let alone Chaucer, and their knowledge of poetry is very sketchy.' These teachers saw no contradiction in going on in the next breath to describe how, with their best A-level students, they use first-year university papers to guide first-year sixth-form work.

It is easy enough to make monkeys of people by using their dottier statements. But there is a serious point. For how many children is it 'better' to read Chaucer, or indeed Caesar, than to learn to cull from your neighbourhood the history of its past and turn that into words which evoke period and passion? For any? For a few? For most? If for any, which? It is surely not harder to learn critically to dissect a great text than it is to write a play that will work for an audience.

The academic, traditional way is certainly 'better' in that it secures university places. But that may not mean more than that our society rewards young people with certificates, and as a result with life chances, for a rather narrow set of attainments.

As soon as these issues are raised, warning signs begin to flash. Like Pavlov's dogs, the many and well-placed defenders of academic traditions rush for the dismissive epithets: 'sloppy rubbish', 'levelling down'. 'The pleasure for the able of academic learning' and 'the scholarly tradition' become rallying cries. The tangle of values in which the comprehensives are caught becomes visible.

The country is short of skilled craftsmen and technicians as well as of successful industrial managers and producers. We are, it seems, very unsuccessful at producing these people. The country is not short of professors of classics or English. It is not even short of inventors. It now has a school system which could produce clever young people familiar with practical and applied skills. But whenever schools try to break away from the academic tradition where the education of clever children is concerned, whenever they even raise questions about what that education should contain, they are accused of trendiness, romanticism and lowering standards.

A debilitating schizophrenia in schools is the result. And it makes it hard to do anything well. Standards and purposes are fudged. Concern over standards discredits the purpose without anyone ever having been clear about what the purpose was in the first place. Yet where schools and, within schools, departments are clear about what they are doing and keep their nerve, the results can be startling. Three examples follow.

The first example is from a mixed-sex school taking children from eleven to sixteen, School S. In this school, all craft subjects were compulsory for all children in the first year. They did cookery, sewing, design (which took in woodwork, metalwork and technical drawing), music and art. In the second and third years, those choosing Latin or German took three out of seven, the rest four. The design technology course led to O-level.

On the day I visited the school, the third-year design class, a substantial number of girls among them, had been set the task of making a toy suitable for an eight-year-old. Anything, out of any material – wood, metal, plastic, fibreglass. The woodwork shop, the metalwork shop and the technical drawing room are grouped together and three teachers were in charge of the equivalent of three classes. The children moved from one room to the other, designing, making, testing. A ferris wheel, a toy rifle, and a boat were among the things in production. The boat was a disaster. It wouldn't float properly.

'I told you it was the wrong material. Why won't it float?'

'Well, it's too heavy. I'm going to hollow out the underneath to make it lighter.'

'Why do you think that will help?'

It didn't in the event.

'Why is it like that do you think?'

It was impossible not to compare this favourably with the depressing art rooms of two public schools, School M and a girls' school, School T, neither of which had any woodwork, metalwork, or technical drawing in their curriculum.

In the boys' school, practical subjects were confined to two periods a week, alternately pottery and art, which is mainly drawing. 'I reckon, since most of these boys are going to be professional people, the most useful thing to do is to teach them how to draw reasonably so that they can use it as a relaxation later in their lives. Maybe it will help them be better doctors or barristers,' is the art master's rather depressing view.

In the girls' school there was not even pottery, just drawing and painting and, again, all done in a rather sparse attic. The girls were drawing a plastic pedal bin and a watering can in pencil on white paper, sitting round in a large circle. They want to get as much practice as they can of doing the sort of thing they'll be doing in the exam,' according to the art mistress. She had been there seventeen years. Her real speciality was art appreciation, 'You know, "caves to Picasso" in a year. Just so they won't look stupid if someone mentions Rembrandt.' And at the same time she thought, 'This is a lovely school. I always say it's the last outpost of the British Empire.'

Even the craft class in another boys' public school, School E, which was introducing design in a serious way, did not compare well. The lesson consisted of a carefully prepared lecture/demonstration on fibreglassing which the boys, in gowns and sitting in rows of desks, watched in silence. 'It's the sort of thing,' explained the master, 'you might do if you were mending a yacht.'

The second example is from School L, in its expensive rural area. The school had the sort of clientèle which expects exam results and the sort of staff who believe in comprehensive schools. The result was an unusually hard-nosed progressivism: integrated studies and exam courses for both CSE and O-level designed by the teachers (mode 3) so that they meshed together, making it possible to teach O-level and CSE candidates satisfactorily, in the same classes. The head brooked no argument from parents about who took CSE and who O-level – and, for his pains, lost some pupils hauled away to local private schools when denied the chance to sit O-levels.

The staff, all hired by the present head, were working on their own internal assessment scheme. They had already produced their own integrated science scheme, their own combined humanities course – both of which were compulsory either at CSE or O-level – and they ran their own in-service training for the staff.

The humanities course was assessed on topic work drawn from sociology, economics, politics, religion, history and geography, and included the world of work, the family, and such hot topics as race relations: enough to make traditionalists' hair curl. The course was originally a CSE mode 3 course, but in 1979 it was also examined at O-level by the northern GCE board, the Joint Matriculation Board. School L was one of the schools which did the pilot studies for an exam which is now generally available.

Such trendy things apart, the school offered among its options Latin, German, Spanish – 'We're striving very hard to avoid the impression that Spanish is for the less able' – and design and craft at all levels, including O-level. The craft design course had two parts. The first involved devising, drawing and making something to solve a given problem. The second involved producing tentative solutions to more complex practical problems and modifying existing design solutions to overcome specified snags. Realistically, however, the school warned its pupils, in the leaflet describing the exam courses they could choose, that O-level passes in design and craft would not always be accepted by further education courses which required a certain number of passes for admission.

The best mathematicians in the school had begun to take O-level maths a year early, helped by the staff at lunchtime. They also entered the international maths Olympiads which had been running for twenty-one years. 'It's a bit gimmicky, but it's fun for the gifted children,' the head of maths said.

In short, the whole approach in this school represented a major departure from earlier traditions. The results, when it worked well, showed, for example, in the fifth-year geography. The school followed the Schools Council's 14–18 Geography Project, teaching to O-level and CSE together and deciding only in the fifth year who took what. Written exams accounted for 50 per cent of the marks, while five pieces of course work, each taking two or three weeks, accounted for 30 per cent and an individual study accounted for 20 per cent. The individual studies were done in pupils' and staffs' own time. Staff helped at lunchtime or after school. Pupils did the work at week-ends, during the holidays and as part of their homework.

These studies were based on hypothesis testing. Each pupil had to choose a hypothesis, design the study, carry it out and report the whole process with the findings. One pupil had mapped the range of high order and low order services by interviewing customers at a newsagent (low order) and the electrical goods shop (high order) next door to it in the local town. The findings (the electrical goods customers came from much further afield) were carefully drawn on overlays to the Ordnance Survey may of the area. Another pupil designed a survey to test whether meat retailing has become a high order service in the last five years. The pupil designed the questionnaire, interviewed sixty people in the local shopping centre and set out the results. A third examined Van Tünan's hypothesis that intensity of land use varies with distance from the farmhouse or market. The study of a near-by valley had taken a great deal of research, plodding over the fields, and was immaculately presented with a series of map overlays showing farms, fields, roads, drainage, elevation, use of the various bits of land.

'I am constantly spending time with individuals to see how much theory they understand and then being surprised at the level they reach,' the teacher concerned said. He reckons that the work is of first-year university standard. 'I wouldn't stand a cat in hell's chance of tapping this ability on a course with just a terminal exam. It's the best thing I've done in seventeen years' teaching.'

Project work is often not this good. Nor is project work with senior children, good or bad, the exclusive province of comprehensive schools. In O-level English and history exams, much of the pioneering has been done by independent schools. Project work has, however, been developed mainly in the comprehensive schools as a way of allowing children to work each at their own level. Its development is closely allied to the development of CSE exams which, though used in independent schools, are mainly the product of state schools.

The point of the illustration from School L is that the teachers in this comprehensive, asked for examples which would show what could be done by the top groups of pupils in their school, chose project work. Teachers in a near-by ex-direct grant school, School U, chose long, detailed essays based on textbooks and dictated notes to demonstrate high standards.

The third example is from School J, which took girls from eleven to eighteen from the housing estate fringe of a midland city. The English department was run by an enthusiast who described himself as arriving at the school seven years before, 'full of 'sixties euphoria, committed to mixed ability teaching and continuous assessment. Existing exams threatened and excluded our kids and the really able were killed by the grind.'

When he arrived, six of his nine teachers were probationers. They were all still there. Together they sat up evening after evening designing courses, searching for the books and anthologies they wanted, putting their own together where need be, devising their own project-based exams with the local CSE board and for O-level with the Associated Examining Board.

'Our aim in the first years is to make the subject a delight.' They also plugged the basics: fluency, spelling, punctuation. All the work was topic based. Each topic had its own booklet of extracts, poems, ideas, lists of books. Examples of topics were 'the outsider', 'law and order', 'time', 'fire'. The children set their own homework and did an assessment of their own work. Their self-assessments were often brutally frank.

In the fourth and fifth years, the exam course years, the language work was designed to produce facility in different kinds of writing – business letters, stream of consciousness, reviews, reports, poetry, précis. The literature course changed from using books in a general way to 'analysing them in depth'. The scheme had much greater flexibility than conventional exam syllabuses allow.

The girls could choose any one of twelve books which they then studied for half a term. Choices included *Wuthering Heights*, *The Country Girls*, *Lord of the Flies*, *A Day in the Death of Joe Egg*, *Of Mice and Men*, *Tess of the d'Ubervilles*: 'We've grown away from doing only the working class things. Now we do a lot of classics.'

Everyone did Shakespeare in the fifth year; it was optional in the fourth. And if anyone wanted to do something not on the list, they could, if they could sell the idea to their teacher. One girl was very struck by Mao's death and wrote a 10,000-word study of his life and ideas (extremely well punctuated and spelt). The head of the department had to send it to the local university for assessment since he was not himself qualified to appraise it. It got a very flattering report and was eventually allowed to count for two of the twelve pieces of work which have to be submitted for the exams. One of her other pieces was on the death wish in *Anna Karenina* – her own choice of book and theme.

Both the CSE and O-level exams required twelve pieces of work, three on at least two novels, three on at least two plays, three on poetry and three more on anything the pupils liked. In 1977, from a year group of 280 containing only about twenty girls who had passed the 11-plus (which still existed then), over a hundred got both language and literature O-levels, another thirty got CSE grade 1. Such figures precipitated a visit from the AEB's chief examiner since they did not fit the national curve. She took away fifty folders of language work and fifty of literature. The result: she decreed that not enough pupils had been given passes but that too many of those who were, got A's and B's. Some were down graded and some pushed up. The head of department was not pleased by the whole episode: 'I sometimes think they don't want people to be so good.'

Reading the essays of fifth-year pupils on that text of our time, *Lord of the Flies*, the correctness of the English, the economy and clarity with which the girls expressed what they thought about the book, and dealt with the symbolism and the moral implications, was striking. The essays made much fresher reading than the meritorious essays on Conrad gathered up from the first-year sixth form of public school, School M. These were efficient, long and detailed, but they did not spring from the page, they did not suggest any triggering inside the writer's head of a whole chain of thought and insight. Unfair, no doubt. Theirs was a first piece of work on a new book, the other was written after studying the novel for some weeks.

The head of the department in the comprehensive staunchly defended his approach. Given good teachers, he said, there needed to be nothing lowbrow about such methods. As if to make the point, he had put, on the end of a 1,600-word philosophical essay on morality which one fifteen-year-old had done off her own bat, 'Read *Steppenwolf*, Herman Hesse; *Billy Budd*, Herman Melville; *The Outsider* and *The Rebel*, Albert Camus; *Nausea*, J.-P. Sartre.'

Now, by way of contrast, I want to describe things which struck me as excellent in the selective sector and thereby to paint in the other side of the 'difference'. They depended, first of all, to a great extent on homogeneous grouping.

The first example is of a direct method French lesson in the boys' grammar school, School Q. Here thirteen-year-old boys were enacting with relish a scene at Orly Airport when a customs man catches a watch smuggler, part of the *Français d'aujourd'hui* course developed by Manchester Grammar School.

They'd been working on this topic for two weeks. First a slide/tape run-through, then the scene was played. No shortage of volunteers or of thespian talent. The smuggler duly apprehended and removed, the officer and his chief were next subjected to an impromptu press conference by the rest of the class. Homework assignment: to write a front-page newspaper story of the incident and lay it out complete with headlines, pictures, captions.

The willingness of the boys to take part even with a

stranger like myself busily scribbling on a pad at the back of the room and the competence with which they got their tongues round colloquial expressions after, for most of them, only five terms of French suggested that language teaching was not yet dead. That school, which did not take boys until twelve, got virtually all its pupils (they were the top 26 per cent from the local primary schools) through O-level French in the first term of the fifth year.

The second example is from a large boys' prep school, School V. Fifteen thirteen-year-olds, due to take scholarship exams in a couple of weeks, were being led at breakneck speed through their maths revision. 'A lot of these boys could do O-level the same day and probably get grade A's,' was their master's view, expressed in a sort of rapid-fire telegrammese. 'Not a trained teacher, myself, of course.'

The lesson proceeded with a series of examples. 'Now this roll of paper, used in a hard winter to cover the tennis court, spray it every couple of hours when there's a hard frost. Decent skating rink in about three days. Diameter of core ... diameter of roll ... I've measured those, that's roughly right, not exact but it'll do. Length ... Now how thick is the paper?

'Next one. Gramophone record. Bit in the middle ... centimetres, bit with the grooves ... centimetres diameter. Again these figures are approximate but not entirely rubbishy. Plays for half an hour and goes round at $33\frac{1}{3}$ revs per minute. See if you can write down the expression for the number of grooves. Now actually, of course, it's all one groove in a spiral. Would the groove reach the river if it was laid out straight? In other words; how long is it –?' He works it out for them on the board, using all kinds of short cuts. 'Never do that. Very bad practice.

'Now linear equality. This is potty. But if you haven't seen it before you're bound to make a hash of it ...' And so on.

Such a class of thirteen-year-olds – none of them spoke a word throughout – would not be possible in a comprehensive school. It raises the whole question of how valuable so high a level of performance is at this age, and how necessary the companionship of others like them is for children capable of it. An extremely high level of ability in maths is often put in the same category as dancing and music, which need early identification and specialization. Sir Cyril Burt campaigned for special schools for brilliant mathematicians, and so has Lord Snow, arguing the importance of creating a 'critical mass' of able children. The evidence is, however, ambiguous, as was shown by a study Professor Eric Hoyle and Mr T. Christie carried out for the Public Schools Commission in 1970 (page 133).

Precociousness in maths is one area which, in large numbers of comprehensives, is both recognized and provided for. At Sutton-in-Ashfield, for example, the inspectors found a fourth-year pupil taking A-level. At one of the schools I visited, a boy was being taught by special arrangement with a near-by university, 'because we just couldn't teach him any more'. Extra maths, like Latin, is the vehicle for extracting and advancing the brightest groups of children in many comprehensives. None the less, the slowness with which bright children progress in maths in both primary and comprehensive schools must be a major source of worry. Parents with children in comprehensives can, if they choose to compare, see at a glance in very many cases the great difference in the amount of maths covered by, say, thirteen-year-olds in independent schools and their own children. It requires of them a real act of faith not to be rattled by this.

The third example of the sort of area in which the independent sector has the edge over comprehensives is rather different. It is of the remedial O-level English class in boys' public school, School E (which is mentioned on page 23). The school was not one of the most academic, but when IQs were tested on entrance, none were below about 108. The school was strictly streamed and half the bottom form of twenty-nine were usually 11-plus failures, refugees from a secondary modern fate. The master who taught half this bottom class for English was described by his headmaster as 'a quite marvellous teacher of stupid boys'. He himself described the boys as 'a group who don't think of themselves as very bright'. Small wonder. Their report cards, which were filled in by all their teachers once a fortnight, contained this sort of comment from other teachers: 'struggling'; 'wake up'; 'not impressed so far'; 'hasty, concentration must be 100% or you will fall behind', 'weak test: fair essay, more OOMPH needed'; 'goonish, could do better.'

To these, somewhat incongruously, the English teacher, who was also their form master, had added such comments as, 'I like the look of this. Well done'; and, 'If he can keep this up all will be well in July.'

'The most important thing is to keep up their morale,' he said. A hard job when, for example, chemistry 'prep', which was on worksheets comparable in scruffiness to any comprehensive, was slashed through and marked in large letters, IDIOT and FOOL.

The class started with a snap test, mainly spelling. 'Right, gentlemen; a piece of paper please. Received, abysmal, accept, argument – 6·2 of you got that wrong yesterday – their, its [these he put in sentences], Who were the school's founders? What did the first line of the Hal/Falstaff scene show?' And so on.

They then read a short story by Hemingway, 'The End of Something'. 'I thought we'd give *Henry IV* a rest today.' The teacher read, stopping from time to time to ask what they thought something meant. They discussed it rather haltingly but with evident enjoyment. They had written short one-page essays the day before for 'prep' on 'tiredness before half term'. 'I think I can honestly say School E and its routine are getting the better of me.' 'Half term, half term, the period of relaxation, the gathering of strength and the paradise sandwiched between twelve weeks of hell.' The spelling was pretty bad, so was the picture of the school which emerged.

These boys would get an average of 6·5 O-levels. That group always did. They would almost certainly not get anything like it in a comprehensive. And that was what their parents paid for. 'I think perhaps we do spoon-feed them too much. At the bottom, not at the top, of course, there simply is not the time for them to understand each thing and to master the syllabus as well. For them the purpose of O-level and A-level

69

is partly to get the tickets they need. This is what the universities and employers want. Also, passing exams gives them confidence that they are the sort of people who can pass things. They sometimes do surprisingly well at A-level. Everyone is under academic pressure here. They all feel exhausted by half term but I think I can safely say, with the exception of one master who has left, we never had anyone push so hard that we've had chaps crack over exams.'

In the prep school, School V, where they did not take pupils who they thought had not got the potential to get O-levels, the slowest were described as 'incredibly stupid'. In the grammar school whose French was such fun, they ran an elaborate system to chase up, cajole, support and bully anyone who did not turn in adequate homework dead on time. In comprehensives, these children with IQs of between 100 and 110 are the solid middle of the school. They are not regarded as marginal in any sense, and they would not be nursed through public exams in at all the same way. Nor would they ever be described as stupid. After all, CSE grade 4 is notionally what an average child would get if all children entered CSE exams. That is, way below any O-level.

This difference in position goes all the way through the schools, and it is perhaps the main thing that worries parents of children who are just above average. 'In the past,' said a teacher in the sixth-form college, School R, nostalgically, 'marginal A-level students would have been trained.' In the present, such pupils will probably fail. When they do they will not have the extremely valuable, door-opening certificates, even if the crammed knowledge which acquires them is almost valueless.

'I think,' said the head of a boys' public school, School W, when asked whether school like his spoon-feed, 'the more intelligent benefit from being told to go off and find things out, being encouraged to do their own research. But people who are less bright and imaginative feel much more confident if they are given notes and know where they are. Launching them into the jungle of projects and research can lead to a number going under.'

A girl who moved from a state school to the girls' independent day school, and who still saw her old friends around town, put it this way: 'They just don't have to work. They're mostly only taking one or two or maybe three O-levels and it's not because they're thick. I know they could do it, but they don't have to work. When I was in middle school we used to have these projects: I never did anything until the last minute, then I'd just copy a couple of sides out of a book. No one ever said anything.'

The question raised is more complicated and more important than simply one of expectations being too low in comprehensives – though that is part of the problem. If schools like these selective and independent ones are pushing young people through the public exams and into the universities, are they, in national terms, in some sense stealing the places of bright children taught in different ways or pushing them into less desirable places?

The headmistress of the midlands girls' comprehensive, School J, felt strongly that this was so. At the same time, she did not think the answer was to try to do the same. 'The sort of work they do here now is so much more interesting than school work used to be, though I suppose it is not so rigorous. But then I ask myself, do we have the right to put a youngster through such pain and grief? If they are bright, the stuff is there. They can reach for it. To put pressure on children which makes them unhappy is terrible. Yes, they must be pushed. Adolescents have to be – and want to be – but they must have some independence too.'

This difference in attitude was stated again and again by comprehensive teachers, 'We can only nag so much.' 'We can only make sure that if they want it it's there.' 'In the end you cannot force people to work however clearly you can see that they could do better.'

There is inevitably in the comprehensives a new voluntary element to learning for clever children. They cannot be flung out for failing to make the grade. There are many around them of less ability among whom they can hide. While clubs and societies in comprehensives offer many clever children a way of pursuing their interests to a more specialist level in their early secondary years, no one will force them to join.

'There is,' to quote one deputy head, 'a lower centre of intellectual gravity in comprehensive schools.' Schools can to some degree counter this by raising levels of expectation and improving punctiliousness over records, assessment, marking and homework so that good workers at any level have the security of not being freaks or feeling they are working unnoticed. But it is impossible by definition, below the sixth form, for comprehensives to re-create the studious, academic atmosphere of the best selective schools. Where conformity brought rewards before, a higher premium is now set on more eccentric qualities. The 'successes' turned out into the world are likely to be rather more self-motivated people than were some of the 'successes' of the old system.

Realizing this potential in the comprehensive system depends, however, on a cool nerve. There has been in recent years a barrage of complaint about standards of literacy and numeracy among the mass of school leavers. Schools have already concentrated a high proportion of their resources on the lower ability children, as was seen in Chapter 1. That tendency is getting a further boost from central government.

The Assessment of Performance Unit, set up by Margaret Thatcher when she was Secretary of State for Education and Science, has begun to operate as a barometer of standards, but not the sort of standards which monitor the imaginative burgeoning of intelligent children's talents. The first survey they carried out in May 1978 tested the maths of a national sample of eleven-year-olds. The second, in November 1978, tested the maths of fifteen-year-olds. Language (English) testing began in 1979. Science will be tested in 1980. Over time, these surveys will provide some indication of whether national standards are going up or down. They are likely to act as a powerful incentive, driving them up by tacitly encouraging schools to concentrate on the skills that are tested. This development of testing is not necessarily going to be a good thing for clever children. It is much more likely to add further impetus to the phenomenon already observable of concentrating on the lower levels of ability.

There have been warnings, particularly with reference to primary schooling, from the head of Her Majesty's Inspectorate, Sheila Browne. In a speech to the Council of Local Education Authorities in July 1977, she said, 'The recent swing towards the basic skills ... seems to be leading to a narrowing of the definition of these skills and a risk of separation of these skills in the curriculum from their application.' School, in other words, becomes narrower and more boring. The message is by implication though not explicitly reinforced by the HMI primary survey, *Primary Education in England* (1978).

In such a climate, the fate of the bright comes more than ever to depend on the teachers, for it is they alone who can make the difference between boring slog, debilitating time wasting, and stimulating and exciting work solidly based on essential intellectual skills. There is a real risk, in secondary as in primary schools, that concentration on basic skills for those of lower ability will result in a serious narrowing of school experience and in less competent or energetic teachers taking refuge in simply satisfying test requirements instead of striving for the rather amorphous but none the less enriching elements of education.

The risk is the greater because continual sniping has seriously undermined the comprehensive school teachers' confidence and consequent ability to promote with conviction the value of a broad general education. The undermining has been greatly assisted by the ease of finding shoddy standards of work in a great many hard-pressed schools. It is only a small jump from saying a thing is badly done to saying it is a bad thing to do. There is every danger that this jump will now be made. If it is, much of great value, much that is exciting and promising, could be destroyed, leaving a very dreary prospect indeed for bright children in state schools: schools increasingly dedicated to dragooning the majority through narrow tests.

It would be a paradoxical outcome for a move designed to

improve standards. The danger of it occurring is increased by misplaced pessimism, but it is also increased by too great romanticism. Too rosy a view encourages sloppiness and sloth, a feeling that the job is easy and any formal accountability an insult and a blight. The best antidote to complacency is contemplation of national statistics. Dry and depressing they may be, but they are the only barometer of how things overall are going.

The next two chapters are therefore devoted to sorting out truth from fiction in observable national trends. First, overall levels of performance. Secondly, changes in particular subjects and in access to higher education.

3 The National Picture

What evidence, if any, is there about academic standards in comprehensive schools overall? It is a partial question since it ignores music, craft subjects, behaviour, social tolerance, the myriad other justifications advanced for comprehensive schooling. It ignores the value that should be placed on the sort of differences described in the last chapter. But schools cannot afford to hide from the central charge behind a barricade of counter-claims. The inculcation of academic skills is one of the only purposes of schooling on which virtually everyone agrees.

When the idea of comprehensives was espoused it was widely claimed – particularly by many Labour party supporters – that the benefits of a grammar school education would thereby be made available to all. A new and different form of education was not the main objective. More of the best then existing was the goal. It is therefore fair to ask how far the numbers reaching high academic standards have been increased by the change and if they have not, why not.

The acrimonious public debate about standards is mainly conducted in terms of public examination results, much as this infuriates those who regard pursuit of certificates as irrelevant or distorting to education. Certificates are demanded by our society as its only available measure of ability and application, and schools which fail to help those of their pupils who can gain these accoutrements to do so, fail them utterly. It will not do to dodge the argument about exam performances. But it should at the same time be lamented that there are not equivalent measures for pupils' breadth of understanding or social tolerance, or intellectual curiosity, which might contribute to a wider picture.

The academic argument falls into two main parts: the *exams argument* – raw figures for passes and what those passes mean in terms of constant standards and different subjects and *access to higher education*, an argument which is about values and motivation as well as success. This chapter will deal with overall national trends in so far as they are discernible. The next will look more closely at particular subjects and complaints and at biases in patterns of higher education.

The exams debate itself resembles most closely in its abstruseness those medieval theological arguments about the number of angels which can be accommodated on a pin's head – except that it matters more. Such evidence as there is is patchy and contentious. Nothing is certain.

In Manchester for example, both the A-level pass rate and the numbers entering for A-level have been falling fairly steadily for ten years in county schools. In 1964, 70 per cent passed, in 1977, just over 56 per cent. Manchester went comprehensive in 1967 in all except its Roman Catholic schools.

In Oxfordshire, which went comprehensive piecemeal between 1965 and 1974, both numbers and percentage passing A-level went up in 1976. In 1974, 2,809 candidates entered the exam and 67 per cent passed. In 1976, 3,071 entered and 74 per cent passed.

Both Manchester and Oxfordshire's results have usually been attributed more to population changes than to changes in standards. But, early in 1979, the case against Manchester was greatly strengthened. R. W. Baldwin, chairman of the governors of Manchester Grammar School and a member of Manchester Education Committee, circulated to the newspapers an analysis of results from Manchester and from the neighbouring borough of Tameside. Tameside is the education authority which came to national prominence by reversing plans to introduce comprehensives, defying the Secretary of State for Education and Science, then Fred Mulley, and winning their case in the courts.

Tameside and inner Manchester are not very different in terms of the social background of children. The comparison showed Tameside's schools, grammar schools and secondary

oderns together, getting 23 per cent more passes in O-level
CSE grade 1 and 52 per cent more in O-level alone. In
odern languages at O-level, the lead was 245 per cent, in
aths 79 per cent, in English 41 per cent. The figures also
owed Tameside pupils getting 9 per cent more A-level passes
t 31 per cent more passes at grades A to C. In modern
nguages, the A-level lead in Tameside was 144 per cent, in
aths 82 per cent, in natural sciences 53 per cent.

When Sheffield's first fully comprehensive intake reached
-level in 1974, O-level results declined slightly, but CSE
ade 1s have increased enough to raise the combined GCE
-level/CSE 1 score from an average of 1·89 per pupil in the
st selective years to 2·21 by 1979.

In contrast, a comparison made in 1978 of the selective areas
Buckinghamshire around Aylesbury, Beaconsfield and High
Vycombe with the comprehensive areas around Milton
eynes showed a much higher, and rising, percentage of all
ildren getting one or more A-levels and five or more GCE or
SE grade 1 passes in the selective areas.

But when the results of children's intelligence tests at eleven
the two areas were compared, the picture changed. Families
ith clever children clearly flock to the selective areas. In 1971,
ell over a third of the primary school children in the selec-
ve areas had a score on tests of 108, and 17 per cent were over
18. In the non-selective areas around Bletchley, only a fifth
ere over 108 and only 5 per cent over 118. (The figures
roved so contentious that they were not published.)

In Hertfordshire, the first area of the county to go com-
rehensive, the Welwyn area, has seen a 95 per cent rise in
)-level passes in ten years (four times the increase in popula-
ion), and a 63 per cent rise in A-level passes (almost double
he rise in population).

In Devon comprehensives, the percentage of A-level candi-
lates passing two or more subjects rose between 1975 and
977, overtaking the grammar schools' success rate. But the per-
entage of fifth-year comprehensive children getting five or
more graded O-levels fell while the success rate of candidates
in grammar schools held steady.

The point of these local illustrations is to demonstrate th impossibility of finding conclusive evidence in local example Local cases are bound to be subject to all kinds of specia factors.

Taking the country as a whole, the most telling case again comprehensives was made by Mr Baldwin in an article in th *Black Paper 1977*, called 'The Dissolution of the Gramma School'. Mr Baldwin's writings have involved him in contro versy. The validity of the devices used in this article to co: rect his figures so as to allow for areas where grammar schoo still 'cream off' the most able children have been questioned.

These controversies have distracted attention from Mr Balc win's most useful series of figures. The first table in the *Blac Paper* article showed the change in the percentage of schoc leavers from the whole of the state sector passing exams be tween 1966, when 11 per cent attended comprehensives, an 1975, when 67 per cent did so (Table 1).

TABLE 1

	At least 1 CSE	5 or more CSE passes	At least 1 O-level or CSE grade 1	5 or more O-levels or CSE grade 1	At least 1 A-level	At least 2 A-levels	At least 3 A-levels
1966	16·15	4·82	36·28	17·23	10·88	8·52	5·42
1969	30·11	12·33	44·81	18·13	12·56	9·59	6·04
1970	33·63	14·30	47·55	18·34	12·90	10·02	6·06
1971	34·84	15·37	48·22	18·65	13·68	10·52	6·51
1972	37·20	16·98	49·88	18·37	13·24	10·11	6·34
1973	Comparisons invalidated by raising of school leaving age						
1974	61·45	23·42	58·20	17·84	12·54	9·61	6·01
1975	*	*	*	*	12·51	9·69	6·17

* Figures not yet available.
SOURCE: *Black Paper 1977*.

These figures in the table show a decline in the proportion passing five or more O-levels or CSE grade 1s – usually re garded as the essential level of achievement for able children They also show a decline in the number getting A-levels. These figures have not been disputed. They cover the period of the main reorganization of secondary education and they show a light loss in attainment at the higher ability levels. They also show a steady and substantial gain in the middle range.

Since then, the Department of Education and Science has worked out figures which extend this table to include 1976 (Table 2). These show a slight upturn at A-level, and an even slighter improvement at O-level after another fall.

TABLE 2

	At least 1 O-level or CSE	5 or more O-levels or CSE 1	At least 1 A-level	At least 2 A-levels	At least 3 A-levels
1975	—	17·14	—	—	—
1976	62·51	17·35	12·92	10·19	6·53

SOURCE: Department of Education and Science (privately supplied).

The department declined to extend the figures any further. It now says that Baldwin's table is misleading because it is based on figures which exclude all those who take a mixture of CSE and O-level exams. Their latest figures, which include this group, show very much the same pattern: slight decline followed by the first signs of slight gain.

TABLE 3 *Qualifications of leavers from maintained schools 1969–70 to 1976–7 (England and Wales).*

	Percentage of all leavers from maintained schools with:	
	5 or more higher* grades in O-levels/CSE	1 or more A-levels
1969–70	19·7	12·9
1970–71	20·2	13·7
1971–2	20·2	13·2
1972–3	Comparisons invalidated by raising of school leaving age	
1973–4	19·9	12·6
1974–5	19·3	12·5
1975–6	19·7	12·9
1976–7	20·4	12·9

* O-level grades A–C and CSE grade 1.
SOURCE: Department of Education and Science, *Statistical Bulletin*, 1/78, July 1978.

The figures in Table 3, covering the whole of the state sector in England and Wales, iron out the quirks and variations produced both by the extremely varied pattern of school organization which is now emerging, and by social differences between areas. They are also detached from the partial impressions gained by employers and by those admitting students to higher and further education. Such people's views are influenced by variations in the population applying to them, the sort of thing which caused the managing director of a large insurance company to congratulate the enraged headmistress of the midlands girls' school, School J, on the remarkable improvement in standards in 1977. 'I've just taken on some marvellous girls,' he told her. His firm had just recruited into mundane jobs several sixteen-year-olds with eight O-levels – the school's best potential university entrants.

Compared with figures for the state schools only, national figures for all exam passes in all kinds of schools, state and independent schools and further education colleges, in 1976 showed a slight rise in the percentage of school leavers getting two A-levels compared with 1970, and a similar increase in the overall percentage getting five or more O-levels or CSE grade 1s. Since there has been a slight decline in the state sector, all the improvement must have taken place in independent schools.

This is disappointing and worrying to supporters of comprehensive schools, if it means, as it seems to mean, that the proportion achieving high standards has ceased to rise. It is the more worrying because, between 1960 and 1970 (when there were relatively few sixth forms whose pupils had at eleven entered comprehensive schools), the proportion qualified for higher education rose fast from 6 to over 13 per cent – a phenomenon attributed to the grammar schools.

There is a highly technical argument about whether these static percentages do, in fact, mean a levelling off of achievement for top ability children. First, however, for the other major message from the national figures. There has been a steadily rising number of exam passes among children of middle ability, those who take and pass less than five O-levels or CSE grade 1s. Only 16 per cent of children left school in 1977 without any public exam passes. In 1967, almost half did so. In 1977, 27 per cent of leavers had passed four subjects; in 1967 only about 17 per cent had done so.

Children in this group fell, in the past, on either side of the 11-plus divide, going into the lower streams of grammar schools or into secondary moderns. Secondary moderns that were really good academically were not common, and even though many of the grammar schools which survived modified the way they treated their less able pupils in response to the rivalry of comprehensives, some remained astonishingly bad. One London grammar school, in the year before it finally became a comprehensive in 1977, achieved an average of only 2·3 O-level or CSE grade 1 passes for each pupil.

There are plenty of stories of individual schools where changing from grammar school to comprehensive seems to have directly caused increases in exam passes. School D, in the north-east, had an excellent reputation as a grammar school, yet they found, when their first group of comprehensive pupils reached O-level in 1977, children who would never have got into the school when it was a grammar school passed four O-levels. Many more of those pupils than of the previous grammar school pupils came from working class homes and immigrant families. Yet 7 per cent of the grammar school pupils used to leave without four passes at O-level. Another ex-grammar school now gets double as many children through five subjects as it used to before it went comprehensive.

It would be wrong to generalize from such stories. If all comprehensives had been as successful as these two, the national figures for five or more passes would show an increase. They do not. Each school's performance is different. Some have done well, some badly. To make any judgement on the quality of what each school is doing, exam results have to be carefully related to the measured ability and social background of the children, for, however hard a school may try to overcome handicaps, these things do greatly affect children's academic results.

The most useful pragmatic check is to superimpose a school's exam record on the intelligence range of its pupils. It is a dangerous business. Research by Alice Heim has shown that if a battery of tests each concentrating on different skills is used in the couple of years before public exams are taken, the correlation for individuals between test results and exam success is high. But when the gap is five years, the tests and the testers many and various, predictions for individuals based on these sorts of test are extremely unwise.

That said, without knowing what the spread of measured intelligence is in a school, its results are impossible to assess. Peter Newsam, Education Officer for Inner London, reckons, as a quick rule of thumb, that a London school ought to show five times the number of O-level/CSE grade 1 passes as it has children in the top ability band. The top band in London schools is defined as the top 25 per cent of the city's children. (London children scored below average on verbal reasoning tests throughout the late 1960s, and early 1970s, so that London's top 25 per cent is equivalent to a broader band of ability nationally.) Such rules of thumb are important if crude. Some London schools, for all that they are called comprehensives, have in their older classes almost no children in this top band.

London schools, because of the system used to allocate primary children to secondary schools, have a record of IQ scores. Many schools have no record of their children's intelligence test scores. Others make it an article of faith not to plot out the distribution of their intake in this way. But, by and large, with all schools, the better the results look, the more likely schools are to flourish them. The girls' independent school, School T, in which the lowest intelligence test score was about 110, not surprisingly made much of getting 90 per cent through eight O-levels. The boys' public school, School E, with a similar intake, was understandably proud of getting all its boys (except for two or three dropouts) through two A-levels even if a fair number got grade E's.

Coyness about exam results is grounds for suspicion. 'I'm afraid I don't seem to have a copy of last year's results. Someone must have taken it out of my file,' said the head of a

rammar school, School X, which takes the brightest quarter
f the local primary school children in an area of the country
here intelligence test scores are well above the national aver-
ge. When he found the figures, they showed that the school
ot not much more than half its pupils through five O-levels.

Reticence is more excusable in schools which have very few
ever children. Results look terrible, and explaining them is
omplicated. For example, in one large comprehensive, School
, in 1978 only ten children got six or more O-levels or CSE
rade 1 passes out of a fifth-year group of 360. Results were
deed bad, but not quite as bad as they sound. The school
ad only seventeen children in the fifth year who had come
a the top 25 per cent primary school intelligence tests at
even. The school did get 293 O-level or CSE grade 1 passes
together.

This school was probably more typical than the two very
uccessful comprehensives formed from grammar schools
uoted before. In general, the large number of 'new' O-level
nd CSE passes seem to be distributed among a wide band of
hildren. The impression is, that while many achieve some
uccess, too few get a solid and even grounding across the main
ubjects.

Since 1952, the number of candidates taking O-level has
isen by over five times. But the average number of subject
ntries for each candidate has fallen from more than five to
ess than three, and the average number of passes from over
hree for each candidate to less than two. Many more people
re entering, many of them in only a few subjects.

In the years between 1961–2 and 1974–5, the proportion of
ll school leavers who passed O-level or CSE grade 1 in maths,
nglish, a science and a modern language, often regarded as
he four essential elements of a well-balanced education, rose
rom 7 per cent of all boys and 5 per cent of all girls to 9 per
ent of all boys and 10 per cent of all girls. But all the im-
rovement was before 1968–9. From then on, the boys fell
ack one percentage point while the girls improved one per-
entage point.

This patchy performance does not necessarily mean that

schools are moving to easy options in order to clock up lots of passes. During the five years between 1969 and 1974, for example, when the relevant age group rose by 8 per cent, passes in Latin fell by a quarter but passes in physics rose by a quarter. (Figures submitted to the House of Commons Select Committee on the Attainment of School Leavers.) It is more likely that schools are allowing a patchy pattern of achievement to develop because of their determination to encourage everyone to do the things they are good at. In the process, they may be neglecting to push the bright through the things they ought to master whether they are good at them or not.

The part, if any, that comprehensive reorganization of itself has played in increasing the number of exam passes overall cannot be disentangled from other changes which have taken place at the same time. The school leaving age was raised in 1973–4 to sixteen, meaning that for the first time the compulsory leaving age more or less coincided with the first public exams. The effect on exam passes is clearly shown by Mr Baldwin's figures to have been immediate and dramatic.

CSE exams were only introduced in 1965, providing public exams for a whole group of people who had not taken them before. O-level is notionally intended for the top 20 per cent of children in any subject. CSE is notionally designed to cater for the next 40 per cent. The rising proportion of children taking the exam is probably as much a function of its newness as anything else.

Furthermore, there is need for caution over what is being achieved. Anything below a grade C at O-level would once have been counted as a fail where now it yields a piece of paper, even though it is not regarded as a pass. On top of this, over 20 per cent of those taking CSE get lower than grade 4. A grade 5 means generally about 20 per cent success in the exam, though it varies greatly. It is not an impressive qualification.

A third factor making it hard to tell what has been happening is that there is no such thing as a fixed standard in public exams against which performance can be measured. With all but the simplest yes-or-no types of exam, standards depend upon the subjective judgement of the examiners and on the grading policy of the examining board.

During the time in which the number of candidates for O-level increased fivefold, the pass rate remained almost steady at around 60 per cent. Examining boards are extremely reluctant to say that they have a policy of passing around two thirds of their candidates. They point to pass rates in particular subjects and particular years which fluctuate considerably. But the fact remains that, over twenty-five years, taking all boards together, the percentage of all candidates passing has remained constant.

The arrival of CSE exams in 1965 did little to change this pattern, though it had been supposed that CSE would remove the weaker candidates from the O-level entry and that, as a result, the O-level pass rate would rise. This did not happen. Instead, more and more people have entered for O-level. With a constant standard it might be expected that greater numbers entering would produce a lower pass rate. This did not happen either.

There are several possible explanations. First, a whole new group of children began to take public exams. These new candidates could have been simply of the same standard as the previous candidates. If this is so, something has put an end to a large-scale waste of talent. The rise in passes began well before the raising of the school leaving age and has coincided with the change to comprehensive education.

Secondly, it is possible that the examination boards have deliberately kept the pass rate at about two thirds. Given the difficulty of keeping a constant standard, some such rule of thumb is more or less inevitable. But it does mean that any idea of a clear standard against which the performance of a type of schooling may be measured is highly questionable. It becomes theoretically possible to flood the market with exam candidates and thereby ensure that more pass than would have done so had fewer entered. It gives substance to the suggestion that some subjects are harder to pass not because they are intrinsically more difficult but because the calibre of the candidates is higher. This is widely believed by teachers to be the case in physics and German. In such a system the appearance of a constant standard is maintained by ensuring that a constant proportion of candidates fail, while the standard is in fact as much a function of the number of candidates entered as of their skill. The standard, while apparently held constant, floats about.

Attention was drawn to the difficulties of assessing change in exam standards over the years by Alan Willmott in his study for the Schools Council, *CSE and GCE Grading Standards: the 1973 Comparability Study*. He compared standards in 1968 with 1973, and showed that, for a given score on an intelligence test, pupils were getting slightly better grades in 1973 than they would have in 1968. This research, first leaked to the press in 1976 by one of the Conservative party education spokesmen in the House of Commons, Keith Hampson, caused a storm. The study was quickly attacked on technical grounds. There was, for example, no way of checking whether the better grades were the result of more lenient marking or of better performance by the candidates. There was no way of knowing whether children were being better taught or whether they were doing better in the subjects they took because they took fewer of them.

Matters are further complicated by enormous changes in the exam syllabuses and in methods of examining in recent years – changes made in response to changed curricula in the schools. Methods of examining have changed because of dissatisfaction with the old-style three-hour papers which assess only part of a pupil's capacity for useful work. Content of courses has changed to accommodate new information and concepts.

In 1974, attempts were made in a joint Schools Council/ Education Department project to compare marking standards with those of ten years earlier. Scripts from 1963 in English, maths and chemistry were remarked by Joint Matriculation Board examiners and compared with scripts from 1973. The results were never published, but it is known that in chemistry at least the exercise proved virtually impossible so great were the changes in the style and content of the exams.

There is, in fact, no clear definition of what the standard of

O-level should be. All the exam boards take elaborate steps to monitor their standards both against previous years and against other boards. But this is their only real guidance. The standard laid down in 1951 when O-level was introduced was that an O-level pass should be equivalent to credit level in the old school certificate. The standard of a school certificate pass was, in turn, defined by circular in 1914 as, 'Such as might be expected of pupils of reasonable industry and ordinary intelligence in an efficient secondary school.' Custom and practice have been largely left to carry on from there.

The same problems exist over A-level standards. It is widely accepted that A-levels have become, in some cases, much more difficult than they used to be: many people say they are now much too difficult, embracing work which used to be and should still be the province of the universities. This is particularly said of the Nuffield science papers, despite modifications made recently. Yet the percentage of the age group passing A-level has remained roughly static. This seems to suggest that standards may have risen.

The matter is again complicated, as at O-level, by the pass rates. At A-level there are clear guidelines, set by the Schools Council. These specify the percentage of the entry which should fall into each grade, including a 30 per cent fail rate. There are fluctuations in these percentages in individual boards' results, particularly in subjects with a relatively small entry, but, by and large, the 70 per cent pass rate is adhered to with remarkable consistency. This indicates even more clearly than at O-level that the difficulty of passing an exam depends on the competition. Crudely, the weakest 30 per cent will fail in each subject be they never so clever. And in theory at least, if a vast army of idiots entered, all the sane, and no doubt some of the idiots, would pass. Physics, generally taken only by the brighter, will be harder to pass than sociology. An A-level from a board drawing many clever candidates could be harder to get than one from a board with average clients – though it should hastily be said that the Associated Examining Board which draws substantially from further education does have a higher fail rate than others.

The existence of twenty-two exam boards examining sixteen-year-olds, (seven for GCE, fourteen for CSE and the combined Welsh board) and eight examining eighteen-year-olds complicates research designed to establish comparability between the various boards. The Schools Council is responsible for comparability and has commissioned some research on it, and the boards themselves arrange for sample scripts to be cross marked. This is not easy. In English, for example, one board may give its highest priority to correct spelling and punctuation, another to evocative writing, another to detailed knowledge of texts. Studies of comparability in single subjects across all GCE boards began in 1978, and it is possible that these will in due course throw some objective light on a tricky field and illuminate the generally held belief that some boards are easier than others. As Dr Clifford Butler told the House of Commons Select Committee on the Attainments of School Leavers in 1977, 'It is well known in the teaching trade ... that one or two of the boards are tough and one or two of them are less hard. It is very difficult to substantiate this feeling by proven research.'

What this can mean in practice is illustrated by a head who, when head of maths in a large comprehensive some years ago, raised the school's success rate at A-level by an average of two grades simply by switching from the small Southern Universities Joint Board, where the A-level maths entry was heavily dominated by Bristol's highly academic selective schools, to the London University Board with its very large, heterogeneous clientèle. Such examples may give rise simply to cynicism. But the questions are really more complicated. A highly successful secondary modern like School F in the home counties uses three different GCE boards along with its local CSE board in order to fit exams nicely to the courses which school's staff have designed. Is it manipulating the weaknesses of the exam system so as to scrape the best results for weak candidates, or is it sound educational sense to design the course first around educational objectives and then to select from the wide range of exams available those that best suit the aim? The matter is one where objective judgements are not possible.

Given all of these complications, pronouncements about standards are extremely unsafe. However, from the figures and from tramping the schools, I have the impression that the rise in certificated achievement for the middle ability children does owe something to comprehensive schools rather than only to the invention of new certificates and the lengthening of school life. But I have the impression, too, that this gain has to some extent been achieved at the expense of the brightest students.

This possibility is clearly illustrated by maths and intelligence test scores from a middle school, School C. In two successive years, pupils whose scores on an intelligence test showed slightly more of them to be average or above than below average, produced scores on a maths test which were exactly the other way round. More came out below average. The cleverer children all scored below the level expected from their intelligence test scores while the stupider ones scored above.

Even at sixth-form level, the same may be true. At the sixth-form college, School R, the proportion of A-level candidates getting A's and B's together is rising, but within that group those getting A's is falling.

More reliable evidence of this phenomenon appeared in 1978 when Richmond-upon-Thames released exam results for the whole authority. The pupils who took O-level and CSE exams in 1978 in Richmond were the first group not to have sat selection exams but to have gone instead into comprehensive secondary schools. The results showed a 57 per cent increase in CSE passes compared with the year before, and a 10 per cent increase in O-level entries. The O-level candidates did not, however, get any more passes than had O-level candidates the year before. More interestingly, though there was a rise of 22 per cent in the number of CSE grade 1s, there was a 36 per cent fall in O-level grade A passes. This is the first time that a redistribution of success has been clearly visible in the statistics. In 1979, O-levels decreased and CSEs increased, but A grades were well up, CSE 1s down.

Support for the idea that higher general performance goes hand in hand with a lowering of the highest performances comes from a major international study. The International Association for the Evaluation of Educational Achievement, based in Stockholm, published in 1976 a summary by David A. Walker of studies of six subjects in twenty-one countries, entitled *The IEA Six Subject Survey: an Empirical Study of Education in Twenty-one Countries*. This showed that while different school systems produced comparable proportions of high achievers, the less selective, long-established comprehensive systems produced more of reasonable standard and less very high fliers. 'High selectivity,' the study concluded, 'minimizes failure and low selectivity maximizes success.'

To sum up: the debate about standards is highly technical and highly contentious. It has not yet produced any very clear answers to what is happening. This is perhaps just as well. While a drop would be inordinately depressing, a rise might foster complacency. And complacency would not do half as much to raise standards as do allegations of collapse – even if there is no evidence to support them. For whatever lack of agreement there may be about whether or not standards have got worse compared with past years, there is a general consensus that they are not high enough.

4 Sectional Views

Worry about academic standards in comprehensive schools is being whipped up, irrespective of what the national figures show or do not show, by the special pleading of particular groups. Employers and university people complain about the apparently declining standard of their recruits. Harry Judge, Director of the Oxford University Department of Educational Studies, stated as a recognized fact in an article in *The Times Educational Supplement* of 23 March 1977 that there was 'a deeply worrying decline in academic standards', which, he suggested, will begin to show up in national statistics as the newly reorganized secondary schools grow out the academic tops they inherited from the old grammar schools.

There is already, in Dr Judge's view, a widening gulf in academic achievement between the independent and the state schools, which could reverse the slow process visible since the war whereby the percentage of children in independent secondary schools has crept down and, with it, the proportion of places in top jobs and prestigious universities going to these pupils.

The loud complaints of employers can be dealt with shortly. The recruits generally complained of are not so much the clever ones, most of whom go into industry – if they do so at all – as graduates. They are school leavers recruited at sixteen or eighteen. What has happened in the last fifteen to twenty years is that the field of potential recruits at this level has changed. The expansion of higher education in the 1960s and 1970s has meant that where, in 1960, only 6 per cent of all eighteen-year-olds went on to study full time, in 1976 13 per cent did so. Higher education is taking in many young people who would in the past have looked for jobs when they left school. Employers have to recruit from lower down the spectrum of ability.

The complaints of universities are at least in part a result of the same thing. They, too, are taking in a broader range of young people. But their complaints tend to take the form of specific allegations about declining standards in particular subjects, usually maths and modern languages followed by the ability to write correctly spelt and punctuated English.

In maths, firm evidence of slipping standards is thin. The Institute of Mathematics and Its Applications conducted a survey among fourth- and fifth-year school children in 1977. The children took a short test. The results revealed the low standard of simple mathematics attained by average fifteen-year-olds. It is expected that this gloomy picture will be reinforced as the Department of Education and Science's Assessment of Performance Unit publishes the results of its tests carried out since 1978.

These studies provide the prophets of doom with plenty of ammunition, but it is important to realize that they do not prove anything at all about changes in standards. They cannot do so, since there is no earlier data with which to compare the findings. It will not be possible to tell what, if anything, is happening in terms of improvement or decline of standards until the same tests have been carried out over several years.

The House of Commons Select Committee on the Attainments of School Leavers in 1977 heard ample evidence that, whatever the comparison with former years, students did not have the sort of maths needed to cope with modern higher education courses. The Association of University Teachers (AUT), giving evidence to the select committee, complained of the varied mathematical background of students which made it necessary to put on special remedial courses in the first year. This variation they attributed to the large number of different A-level courses in maths (over fifty of them); a slight tendency to settle for lower grades in A-level and, more particularly, the fact that many students for science and engineering courses had no A-level maths. This led them to add their voices to those arguing for a broader sixth-form programme so that all these students would have some maths beyond O-level.

Professor D. A. King summed up their position:

The problem I think, or part of it, is in the fact that more and more disciplines require a greater degree of mathematics ... and it would appear the number of people doing A-levels in mathematics is not going up accordingly ... we would like the schools to do this job for us but we do feel we are asking a lot of them. We are asking them to improve very significantly the situation say twenty-five years ago.

There is some evidence that the schools are responding to this demand. After a bad patch there was, between 1974 and 1977, a 19 per cent increase in O-level and 12 per cent in A-level maths passes and a 29 per cent rise in CSE passes at a time when the number of sixteen-year-olds increased by 2·7 per cent.

The impression that maths is a booming subject is reinforced by visiting schools. For example, one major public school is teaching maths A-level in classes of twenty. It has a total of eighty maths A-level students compared, despite its strong classics tradition, with four doing classics. In one county I visited, maths is the most popular of all A-level subjects.

It looks, in fact, as if the AUT's wish for a broader sixth-form education, with more people taking some maths, is being fulfilled. But the way in which the change is happening will not diminish lamentations from the universities. The number of people taking maths at A-level has risen, but the number taking two maths A-levels, the basic requirement for many maths degrees, has halved in ten years as mathematicians too broaden their sixth-form courses.

Demand as much as anything else may account for the constant complaint at the shortage of maths teachers. The Education Department estimated the shortage of secondary maths teachers at 1,120 in 1976, a substantial increase on earlier years. But this figure is based on the number of maths specialists which schools say they need. It is therefore worth noting that the number of graduate maths and science teachers in the schools went up threefold between 1950 and 1975 while the total teaching force only doubled.

To try to meet this demand, the department launched in 1977 a retraining programme for teachers with A-level maths who are prepared to teach that subject. Investigations by the department had, before this initiative was taken, revealed a significant number of teachers with maths A-level who were not already teaching maths.

In the universities, remedial courses in maths are now quite usual. Their existence tends to be taken as indicative of the failure of the comprehensives – a view to which some of the vice-chancellors have contributed. But is it? Take an example of such a course: at Southampton University there were, in 1978, nine applications for each place to read mathematics, thirteen for each place in engineering, eight for physics on its own and with other subjects, and thirteen for all science places taken together. They are not scraping the barrel. Even so, there are complaints about students' inability to do basic calculations and the engineering and mathematics faculties have jointly designed a do-it-yourself remedial programme and arranged enough time in the first-year programme and enough tutorial help for students to make good deficiencies. All students are tested in their first week at the university, and again at the end of the first year. This programme was set up in 1974, and it has turned out that almost all the students, however good their qualifications in maths, choose to take it, though some get through it at a faster pace than others.

The department now recognizes that this sort of work should have been done before, providing a common base of mathematics for students whose different attainments are attributable to the range of syllabuses and the lack, in some cases, of A-level maths more than to any *type* of school. Much light should eventually be thrown upon the state of maths teaching by the Cockcroft Committee, appointed in 1978 to look into maths teaching in schools. If this committee were to find that, while things were not good enough, they were not demonstrably worse, their report might be received with the same overwhelming silence as the Bullock Report, *A Language for Life.*

That report, while it had many crushing things to say about the state of English teaching and language learning in schools, found no evidence that standards were falling. In schools and local education authorities, the Bullock Report has been well received and has been the occasion for large-scale internal reappraisal, but as far as the general public is concerned, it seems to have had almost no effect on the widespread gloom about standards of literacy.

Yet the Bullock Report itself contained in its introduction a salutary reminder of the persistence of such jeremiads by quoting evidence given in 1921 to the Newbold Committee:

Messrs Vickers Ltd reported 'great difficulty in obtaining junior clerks who can speak and write English clearly and correctly, especially those aged from 15 to 16 years'. Messrs Lever Bros Ltd said: 'It is a great surprise and disappointment to us to find that our young employees are so hopelessly deficient in their command of English.' Boots Pure Drug Co. remarked 'teaching of English in the present day schools produces a very limited command of the English language ... Our candidates do not appreciate the value of shades of meaning, and while able to do imaginative composition, show weakness in work which requires accurate description, or careful arrangement of detail.'

At the higher levels of achievement in arts subjects – that is, among those going to university – the University Teachers testified to the House of Commons Select Committee that standards appeared if anything to have risen.

Despite popular opinion, then, the evidence of declining standards in maths and English is not sound. In languages, the scene is more desolate. And it is also in languages that most blame is being laid at the door of comprehensive reorganization. The figures are depressing.

Numbers passing A-level French fell in absolute terms between 1970 and 1976. Passes in German, though up, were not up enough to hold their place with a rising number of eighteen-year-olds. The number passing A-level Russian fell by a third, leaving only 413 successful A-level candidates in the whole of England and Wales in 1976. At O-level for the same years, when the number of sixteen-year-olds rose by 14 per cent, the number of passes in French rose by only 5.7 per cent, though the number of passes in German rose by 20 per cent. The numbers emerging from university with degrees in languages have fallen dramatically – though combined language and arts courses are growing in popularity.

Her Majesty's Inspectors' reports are full of gloom: 'growing concern is felt for the future of foreign language teaching in our schools', said the HMI background papers for the 1977 'Great Debate' education meetings. 'One major reason for anxiety about the future of language teaching in schools is the declining number of language students in sixth forms ... Concern is increasingly expressed in higher education about the difficulty of recruiting language students.' said *Modern Languages in Comprehensive Schools*, no. 3 in the HMI *Matters for Discussion* series.

The inspectorate carried out a survey of modern language teaching in eighty-three comprehensive schools in 1975. Their report is damning. They found few schools where they considered language teaching was good. In most it was characterized by:

... under-performance in all four language skills by the abler pupils; the setting of impossible or pointless tasks for average (and in particular less able) pupils and their abandonment of modern language learning at the first opportunity; excessive use of English and an inability to produce other than inadequate or largely unusable statements in the modern language; inefficient reading skills; and writing limited mainly to mechanical reproduction which was often extremely inaccurate.

At sixth-form level, 'The usual picture was of ill-read students with limited initiative reaching only poor to mediocre standards.' And generally, 'In all too many language classes there was an atmosphere of boredom, disenchantment and restlessness; at times this developed into indiscipline of a kind which made teaching and learning virtually impossible.'

No one denies the grim state of most language teaching in comprehensives. In School H, a mixed comprehensive of over

,800 pupils with a long-established reputation for language teaching, only forty pupils took French at O-level in 1977 and twenty-three of them failed. In the same school in a sixth form of a hundred there was only one A-level student for Russian, one for German, one for Latin and two for Spanish. It had become too extravagant to timetable these languages, so the teachers, rather than give them up, were teaching them in free periods and at lunchtime. The head of department as a result had only two free periods a week.

But, once again, there is another side to the coin. Where languages were in the past mainly the province of selective schools, now most of the country's secondary schools teach at least one foreign language, usually French, and they teach it in most cases to all but the slowest children at least for the first year or two. There was a 101 per cent increase in the number of CSE passes in French between 1971 and 1977. And Her Majesty's Inspectorate, when they undertook in 1973-4 an inquiry into classics teaching in comprehensive schools, came to the conclusion that classics in some form – and it was most likely to be Latin – was taught in 'something like half the country's comprehensive schools. This may well mean that classics teaching is present in more schools than ever before when it is remembered that it was rare to find any classics in the non-selective schools which formed two-thirds of all secondary schools in the early sixties.'

This is not to deny the dramatic fall in higher-level work in Latin: a 38 per cent fall in A-levels since 1971, and a 17 per cent fall in O-levels during the same years. Why things are bad in language teaching in individual schools – and what might be, and in some places is being, done about it – will be discussed later.

What is important nationally is that languages have generally been specialist subjects, chosen as options. Their decline is not reflected in an overall decline in all exam work. Instead, there has been a switch by the brighter children, the ones who take GCE exams, away from languages. It has happened in all kinds of schools. In 1977, a report from the Headmasters' Conference showed a decline of a third in the numbers studying French, Spanish and German in their schools, the 200 most prestigious boys' independent schools in the country.

Is this switch due to sex bias in subject choice? The relative fall in numbers taking languages is more marked for boys than girls, and is usually attributed to sex typing in mixed schools. As comprehensive reorganization has taken place, the number of single-sex schools has more than halved. Those that remain are more likely to be grammar schools. This makes it difficult to disentangle the effects of co-education and of comprehensives.

In 1973, the inspectorate made a study of sex typing in arts, languages and science subjects in mixed schools, *Curricular Differences for Boys and Girls* (1975). The pattern was clear: in single-sex schools, a higher proportion of boys specialized in arts and languages and a higher proportion of girls specialized in sciences and mathematics than they did in mixed schools. After all, any self-respecting school will want to offer a full range of subjects. In a single-sex school, pupils will be encouraged – even made – to take subjects that are on the timetable so as to fill up classes. In a single-sex school, girls will be pressganged if necessary into taking sciences and boys into taking languages. In mixed schools, classes may be filled anyway by volunteers and there is no particular incentive to force extra children into subjects they do not particularly want to take simply to balance the sexes.

It is usually at fourteen, when subject options for O-level and CSE are chosen, that sex typing appears. Until then, most schools make all their pupils follow much the same course, though practical subjects were often divided into boys' crafts (woodwork and metalwork) and girls' crafts (cooking and needlework) before the passage of the Sex Discrimination Act.

The inspectors found that, the earlier a school lets pupils choose subjects, the more marked the pattern of sex bias becomes. In this respect, the inspectors found that comprehensives were less likely than grammar schools to introduce what they dubbed 'premature specialization' – that is, choices before 13 plus. On the other hand, a survey of *Attitudes of School Leavers*, carried out for the Department of Education in 1975, showed that comprehensive sixth-form girls were more likely to choose languages and boys sciences than pupils in other schools. This may mean little since comprehensives are more likely than other schools to be co-educational.

The HMI data are now five years old, and in those years the women's movement as well as comprehensive reorganization have made considerable progress and co-education has become much more widespread. In 1977, the inspectorate asked the GCE examination boards privately to collect figures for patterns of subject choice in boys', girls' and mixed schools, but these are not yet available. When they are, they will not throw much light on the comprehensive question nor on patterns of early specialization since exam boards do not have the necessary information about schools; but they will show broad patterns.

Piecing together the jigsaw, the most likely conclusion is that the decline of languages is one of the main casualties of co-education. But it is probably also the result of a general move away from early specialization, and – when specialization does begin – of a preference for science.

The prescribed curriculum of public school, School E, is a good example of how this can work for able children on O-level courses in schools of all kinds. In this school, only the fast stream are able to do two modern languages, one of them being an option chosen from geography, geology, German, Greek, Spanish, art and design. All the boys have to do three sciences, French and either Latin or classical civilization ('for those with no Latin, or whose Latin proves after a while to be extremely weak'). But the 'normal stream' has no chance to choose a second modern language before the sixth form.

The complaints of language specialists, whether in universities or in the inspectorate, have to be looked at against the background of the campaign waged against early specialization, which has been singled out as one of the prime causes of a drift away from science. Lord Snow's Rede Lecture, *The Two Cultures and the Scientific Revolution*, in 1959 drew attention to the divide which specialization at school created between arts and science students. Sir Frederick Dainton, until

1978 chairman of the University Grants Committee, has long fought for a broader school curriculum including compulsory maths and science. In 1968, a committee under his chairmanship investigated the reasons for the drift away from science which was causing concern at the time. Early specialization in school was found principally to blame, since it turned a disproportionate number of people to arts and made it impossible for those who opted for arts early to change their minds. This campaign now seems to be bearing fruit. In the 1971 annual report of the Universities Central Council on Admissions (UCCA), Dr Geoffrey Templeman, chairman, was bewailing the lack of applicants for universities generally and for science and engineering in particular. In the 1976–7 report, Dr H. R. Pitt, chairman, noted that, for the third year running, applications to universities generally were up and there was a strong trend to engineering, technology and science. This continued in 1977–8, when engineering emerged as gaining most in popularity, while maths and physics were among those showing the greatest increase. The trend was sustained again in 1979, with computing joining the list of subjects showing large increases in popularity.

The relative decline in languages at university can therefore, like the absolute decline in sociology, architecture and combined and general arts, be taken as evidence not of lower standards among able children but of a switch by those children to other subjects, in particular to science, engineering and business studies.

The most interesting thing about the shift to science generally is that the state schools do better in science than other schools. Thirty per cent of all boys entering university read science subjects. Only 20 per cent of boys from schools belonging to the Headmasters' Conference do so, and that includes the direct grant schools. According to Independent Schools Information Service figures for 1978, 24 per cent of girls going to university read science subjects, but only 12 per cent of those from independent girls' schools. At Oxford in 1978, the state schools, which supply only 47 per cent of the intake, provided 56 per cent of the scientists.

This superiority is perhaps surprising in view of the efforts that have been made by the independent schools to improve their science teaching. Science became a compulsory subject in standard common entrance exams for public schools in 1971. Latin had been made optional in 1968 (though schools still feel the need to explain why candidates are not doing Latin).

There is, however, a discontinuity in the apparent advantage of the maintained schools. Those who do study science subjects to A-level in independent schools tend disproportionately to go on to study medicine – both boys and girls. The A-level requirements for places in medical schools are higher than for any other subjects, so they must be very good.

The question of medical school places raises interesting questions, questions of attitudes as much as attainments. Leaving aside value judgements about whether rich and clever people make good doctors, and sharp questions about why independent school pupils so much prefer to be doctors than pure scientists, the fact remains that independent schools are very good at getting their pupils into these highly sought-after places. This could mean that the state schools' apparent superiority in science is partly a result of the fact that their best people are not quite good enough to squeeze out the independent candidates in the competition for medical school places.

None the less, the state schools' record in science is good at the highest levels, and this success does not seem to be being bought at the expense of improved performance on a broader front. Many secondary moderns offered little science, but, according to the Department of Education and Science, from 1971 to 1977, as reorganization gathered pace, CSE passes increased 81·5 per cent in physics; 163 per cent in biology; 116 per cent in all science and technology. O-level passes rose 31 per cent in biology; 36 per cent in chemistry; 36 per cent in physics (DES *Statistics*, 1977, vol. 2).

Science is, indeed, the one area about which there is considerable confidence. The inspectorate, in one of the papers on science for the 1977 'Great Debate' education meetings, had some criticisms to make of the proliferation of science courses offered in comprehensive schools: the lack of technicians, the shortage of labs in many schools, the lack of science in primary schools, the apparent discrimination against or lack of interest by girls. But they ended up with rare praise:

... the science subjects are in fact well ahead of all others except economics in terms of percentage increase over the period. This is all the more creditable if we take into account the indications arrived at by G. M. Forrest [*Standards in Subjects at the Ordinary Level of GCE*, June 1970, published by the Joint Matriculation Board] that physics and chemistry may be the most difficult of all O-level examinations.

The argument about subjects merges at this point with the larger argument about the success of comprehensives in getting people into higher education. Comprehensives are much more likely to send people to polytechnics than the independent sector. Nearly one in six of those going on to degree courses from comprehensives go to polytechnics, compared with one in twelve from independent and direct grant schools. This may, as suggested in Chapter 2, be some victory for the philosophy so eloquently propounded by Dr Patrick Nuttgens, Director of Leeds Polytechnic – a philosophy of the value of practical and applied learning. It may be the result of the undoubtedly superior opportunities for craft work in comprehensives. But it may be simply second best.

Unfortunately, the evidence is far from clear. The polytechnics do not enjoy a high reputation – with some exceptions, particularly for certain departments – and their staff are not always as well qualified as those in universities.

Since, unlike the universities, there has been no central control of polytechnics and no central admissions system, it is hard to measure what is happening. However, it is clear that some have drifted away from the original intention that they should provide practical and vocational higher education attuned to local needs; education of equal esteem but different character from that offered by the universities. Fastest growth in polytechnics has been in humanities and social sciences, not in engineering, science and technology. And *People in Polytechnics*, a survey by Julia Whitburn, Maurice

Mealing and Caroline Cox, carried out in 1972 and covering twenty-eight of the thirty polytechnics in England and Wales, found that 85 per cent of those on degree courses in languages and literature had failed to get a university place.

Figures gathered by the Conference of University Administrators show that the A-level results of university entrants are far superior to those of polytechnic and other higher education students. The universities are undoubtedly creaming the talent, and though they have become more interested in vocational courses or applied components in traditional courses, the universities have in general been followers not initiators in this respect.

Sir Alex Smith, director of Manchester Polytechnic, has railed against the academic snobbery of the British education system, which, he argues, can create in people 'a dislike for being involved in the processes whereby the country earns its living' (speech to the British Association in Lancaster, 1976).

For generations now, the prevailing influence in education has been the respect given to scholastic and academic abilities. There is nothing wrong with that. What is wrong is the associated value judgement that those who do and make, who design and build, who market and manage, are not worthy of similar esteem. Education has become synonymous with the predominant development of mainly scholastic attributes, and has relegated to an inferior role the rest of the wide spectrum of human talents and abilities that are there to be developed. As such it has taken upon itself a narrow confining interpretation of the whole concept of education, and the country now has a surfeit of the development of analytical and theoretical abilities and of capacity for social commentary and an acute shortage of the development of imagination, ingenuity, inventiveness, enterprise and vision in design, development and manufacture.

Correcting this bias Sir Alex sees as being the job of the polytechnics. It is at least possible that the comprehensive schools are half-way to assisting. They are not, however, being helped by employers. Industrialists complain loudly that the cleverest young people will not work for them. They blame the teachers and the schools. And they mount efforts to change things by lobbying the country's independent schools and ancient universities, offering scholarships and inducements. They do not, they say, care about the subject in which their recruits have qualifications, they simply want the 'best'. And they assume that this is where the 'best' are to be found. Comprehensive schools and polytechnics alike seem to be regarded by industrialists as sources of labour or – and of technical skill, but not of inspiration or leadership.

Polytechnics also fight with one hand tied behind their backs by the grant system. Many of their advanced vocational courses do not qualify for mandatory grants, while all degree courses, no matter how soft an option, do qualify. This makes it inevitably harder to attract good students to practical and vocational courses, no matter what a course's intrinsic merits.

In 1977, a Department of Industry report, *Industry, Education and Management*, criticized the academic bent of the British educational system, identifying it as a cause of the country's poor industrial record. In fact, the percentage of graduates going into industry and commerce (possibly *faute de mieux*), though low, is rising (Manchester graduate survey, 1978).

What seems to escape public comment is that, as the Department of Industry's report showed, polytechnic engineering and science graduates are very much more likely to go into manufacturing industry than are university engineers and scientists. The report comments on the importance of applied skills in making good managers. It commends courses with practical approaches of the kind offered by polytechnics. It catalogues the work done on the class and educational background of senior British management. It recites managers' lamentations about the poor quality of many graduate engineers. It fails to ask the obvious question: are these managers likely to bring out the best in those recruits who are prepared to work for them when their background and attitudes lead them to regard these recruits as second best?

The argument is more subtle than simply discussing how the best minds may be tempted into industry. It must also include consideration of whether a straight line from school to Oxford or Cambridge to management is appropriate even for the 'best'. No doubt celever young people's perceptions could be dramatically changed, as the Industry Department report suggested, if industry paid them more and made their working conditions more agreeable. But that is not the same as looking first for people with inventive genius, and asking whether the traditional academic system is, in fact, doing for industry the job of identification it requires.

It is here that the private sector schools may be having one of their most profound effects in cramping the comprehensive exercise. Parental ambition, as discussed in Chapter 2, is driving independent schools into an ever greater emphasis on academic qualifications, and university as opposed to polytechnic places. The chances of getting one of the most sought-after places seem to be materially improved by attendance at one of the major public schools or one of the erstwhile direct grant schools. Private schools (including direct grant schools now independent) together contain less than 6 per cent of the nation's children, but their pupils make up 28 per cent of all those getting three A-levels, gain over half the places at Oxford and Cambridge and a fifth of all university places.

The proportion of pupils from state schools going into higher education has been rising steadily in this century. Admissions, however, are determined as much by space as by the quality of the applicants. More than 70 per cent of all qualified applicants to universities (that is, those with at least two A-levels grade E or above) now get in somewhere, though not necessarily the place they first chose. Most of the rest drop out because they do not want to take part in the UCCA clearing operation when candidates who have failed to get into the universities they chose are offered suitable places remaining vacant elsewhere. Probably many go to degree courses in polytechnics for which there is no comparable clearing house.

Within this overall picture there is variation. The competition between students is for the best places. Medicine and veterinary science, law, some engineering courses, business studies are top subjects; Oxford, Cambridge and some parts of London University such as Imperial College are among the top institutions able to ask for the best A-level grades. At

Oxford and Cambridge, though the intake from maintained schools has continued to rise slowly, the failure rate of applicants from maintained schools has risen faster than the failure rate from other schools as pressure on places has grown. Nineteen per cent of men entering Oxford in 1939 came from state schools, 40 per cent in 1966, 45 per cent in 1979. But in 1979, only 33 per cent of comprehensive applicants got in compared with 38 per cent of all maintained school applicants and 50 per cent of direct grant school applicants.

It is not clear that rising failure rates are caused by declining standards. The brightest students may not apply, recruiting methods may favour a particular kind of schooling and even a particular kind of person. It is also possible that schools experienced in submitting candidates to Oxford and Cambridge vet applicants more carefully before allowing them to apply.

What does show up in figures from Cambridge (Oxford has no comparable figures, since admissions data are not computerized as Cambridge's are) is that students coming from maintained schools are much better qualified in A-level terms than other students. Of men who finished their degree courses in 1979, about half the maintained school entry had A-level scores equivalent to three A grades compared with only 36 per cent of independent school entrants. Of women, 36 per cent of maintained school girls had a top A-level score compared with 30 per cent of independent school girls. Given this superiority, it is not surprising but still worth recording that maintained school students get more firsts than independent school students.

There is certainly no evidence here that the ancient universities are beginning to bend their entry requirements to let in comprehensive school pupils. On the contrary, the figures bear out the belief, strongly held in comprehensive schools, that Oxford and Cambridge entrance is rigged against comprehensive pupils.

Ironically, even if these two universities did discriminate in favour of comprehensive pupils, there would be no guarantee that more children from manual workers' families would enter the universities. This country compares well with other inustrialized countries in getting a relatively high proportion f working class children (about a quarter of all entrants) into igher education. But this proportion improved very little in he post-war years. And there is now some evidence of falling ack to pre-war levels. In 1974, 15 per cent of male applicants o Cambridge were the sons of manual workers, in 1979, 12 er cent. In this respect, comprehensives may not be helping. here is a marked reluctance among many comprehensive upils to try for Oxford and Cambridge places, and those who o are probably more likely to be the children of university rofessors than of manual workers.

There is now increasing pressure within the comprehensives to play the traditional academic game. Postponing decisions about which children have academic potential, delaying pecialization and streaming in comprehensives cannot really e defended if it means loading the dice against bright pupils n competition for university places, however beautiful the ducational theory behind such practices.

Clear signs exist that comprehensive schooling slows down otential university candidates' academic progress. The age t which young people go to university has been rising slowly uring the 1970s. There are also signs that young people are urning away from higher education altogether. The percentage of all young people going on to full-time higher education fell back in the 1970s, causing official forecasts for higher ducation numbers in the 1980s to be repeatedly revised downwards. Within the totals, university applications, which lumped in the early 1970s, rose again, particularly in 1979, but there were no signs that gains in the university sector vould be enough to offset losses in the polytechnics and colleges of higher education. The cause of this overall fall in the percentage of young people going into higher education is unknown. Unemployment may make people anxious to grab jobs when they can. The reduced numbers of teachers in training nay in itself explain much of the fall. The comprehensives may be in part responsible, either for failing to bring people up to the required standard or for making them sceptical about the value of academic training.

Another possible effect of comprehensive schooling is that it encourages young people not to specialize in the sixth form, but to take a mixture of arts and science subjects at A-level. Guy Neave, in his unfortunately now dated study of comprehensive school pupils at university (it was carried out in 1968), *How They Fared*, found that students who had come from comprehensives were more likely to have studied a mixed set of A-level subjects than were other students. Since then the number of young people taking mixed subjects at A-level has been increasing.

Unfortunately, the UCCA figures show that such students are not popular with universities. Candidates with mixed A-level subjects are very highly represented among those who fail to get into the universities of their choice and therefore take part in the UCCA clearing operation. Yet many people recognize that it is harder work to master three diverse subjects at A-level than it is to master three closely related ones.

All of these trends in admissions to higher education are open to two rather different interpretations. Guy Neave argued strongly that open comprehensive school sixth forms coming after a broad secondary course, offered late developers, many children from working class homes among them, a much better chance of getting into higher education eventually than did more academically streamed schools. A significant proportion of the students he interviewed had failed the 11-plus and had continued to amass O-levels in the sixth form. But, by the time they became students, they had acquired more exam passes than the average student. They also tended to choose science degree courses. Guy Neave also found that the students he interviewed did not consider applying to Oxford and Cambridge because they saw it as an alien place with an alien life style.

On the other hand, Professor Gareth Williams's study, *Attitudes of School Leavers*, carried out for the Department of Education and Science in 1975, showed that a significant chunk of comprehensive sixth formers, more than in other schools, did not think they were clever enough for Oxford and Cambridge. The study showed that those who stayed on in comprehensives to take A-levels were rather less well qualified in terms of O-levels than those in other schools, that they were more likely to go straight to university if they were going at all than to take a year off.

The rival interpretation then would have it that longer staying on, a choice of subjects which is not altogether acceptable to those choosing recruits for higher education, lower aspirations and patchier O-level achievement among those entering sixth forms is the result of bad teaching or a form of education which sacrifices young people's progress earlier in their school careers to the interests of children with less academic ability; that they are being deprived of the chance to spend a fallow year before university because they must struggle to catch up; that they are being put at a disadvantage in the rat race for higher education; that they have chosen science because the competition for university places in science is less great than in arts or medicine, or because they have not been taught languages well enough to have that option.

The two views are not wholly contradictory. Those who develop academic competence early are probably being held back compared with similar pupils in academically selective schools. In this way, the late developers are able to catch up. That is good for the late developer and bad for the others.

If the gains for the late developers are not to be swept away in a backlash created by the resentment of those others (or their self-appointed protagonists), the warnings of those who say that academic achievement is being neglected should be heeded. Those who want to see common schools succeed as more than the producers of factory fodder for a power élite educated elsewhere, must take academic weakness seriously. But they must at the same time ensure that these schools are not forced into giving more than due importance to academic values.

The next chapter looks at possible ways in which national policy can be shaped to assist in achieving this delicate balance. The last chapter examines ways in which schools and local authorities are already working on the job.

5 National Options

In the autumn of 1978, the BBC conducted a survey for its programme, *Parent Power*, which asked parents whether they thought their children were getting a better education than they had themselves. More thought they were than that they were not, and the lower the income group of the parents the more likely they were to think things were better. Only a third of parents from upper income groups (groups which include about a third of the population) thought things were better.

Opinion surveys of this kind do not test reaction to comprehensive schools directly, but they do suggest that those who are currently most discontented with the schools are those who are rich and powerful and likely to assert themselves to some effect. For example, Professor R. V. Jones of Aberdeen University used the occasion of his installation as a charter fellow of the College of Preceptors in 1978 to make a speech of considerable bitterness against the abolition of the 11-plus. The ending of selection by academic ability was, he said, a victory for middle class mothers who could not tolerate the consequences for their dimmer children of an efficient meritocracy promoting people purely by ability.

Clearly the pendulum has now begun to swing back to the clever, back to meritocratic as opposed to egalitarian values. Because the discontented are a minority, the swing should not be allowed to go too far. Controlling it does not necessarily require specific decisions. It is more a question of climate and mood directing the action of head teachers, teachers and administrators in their day-to-day assessment of priorities, for education in this country is a decentralized service with control widely dispersed.

National policy decisions are both shaped by and shape the

revailing mood, endorsing some values, frowning on others.
want now to discuss eight issues requiring national policy
ecisions which could importantly influence the way clever
hildren are treated in schools, and so affect the whole future
f the comprehensive system.

he first of these issues is whether or not some form of selec-
on between schools should be reintroduced below the statu-
ry leaving age. Many would argue that comprehensive
hooling has been introduced hastily and as a result of doc-
inaire egalitarian, socialist political theories, without regard
the educational merit of such a system. There are some in-
ications that Rhodes Boyson, both as opposition spokesman
r education and as a Minister during the late 1970s, was
rrect in warning repeatedly that the chances of advancement
rough schooling for some clever working class children had
een diminished.

Even among those who have no particular fear of egalitar-
n, socialist principles, there are many who will accept that,
the process of reorganization, fine schools have been des-
oyed; that independent schooling, only available to the
ch, has been given a new lease of life; and that academic
uccess has become no less dependent on having the sort of
amily which puts value on high-level academic work. Some
amilies may express this concern by buying school places for
heir children, others support and encourage them through
tate schooling. It is a simple step from here to suggest that the
lever should be separated again from the comprehensives at
ome stage of their school career.

The conventional wisdom up to the 1979 general election
vas that there was no serious question of reintroducing the
1-plus. Its unpopularity was too well remembered. Selection
t eleven was shown convincingly in the 1950s and 1960s to
e wasteful of talent, and in the most pragmatic economic and
political terms it became a liability at that time. Not enough
people, it appeared, were being brought to the level of intel-
ectual competence needed in an advanced industrial society.
Telling four fifths of all children that they were a failure at

the age of eleven was not helping. Distinctions were alread
blurring in the divided system as secondary modern school
gradually increased their O-level and A-level teaching despit
official discouragement. After their introduction in 1964, CSI
courses developed both sides of the dividing line. The grow
ing overlap had made a nonsense of the division.

In 1979 the mood appeared to change. The Labour govern
ment's 1976 Education Act, outlawing selection in schools, wa
repealed. Local authorities which had not gone comprehensiv
shelved plans to do so, and some, like Bexley, began to try
to unpick existing comprehensives. It is not at all clear how
popular such a reversal will prove with voters. In the 197£
local government elections, the chairman of Tameside Coun
cil's education committee, Donald Thorpe, a leader of the cam
paign to prevent the introduction of comprehensive schools
lost his seat against the prevailing swing to the Conservatives
In 1979, Tameside Council went Labour against the nationa'
swing, and when Donald Thorpe tried to get back in a Con
servative ward two months later, he was soundly defeated after
campaigning in defence of grammar schools. In Kingston upon
Thames in the summer of 1978, a poll of parents, conducted
through the education department, showed 60 per cent of pri
mary school parents in favour of ending selection earlier than
the planned date of 1983.

Selection at some point in people's lives is inevitable. Higher
education is, and will remain, selective, and employers will
always choose their recruits on merit. What has again become
an issue is whether selection during the statutory years of
schooling should be encouraged, and if so how it should best
be done. (After sixteen, selection becomes to a large degree self-
selection.)

Inside comprehensive schools there is a considerable amount
of sorting and selection already. At fourteen, if not before,
children are sorted into groups for public exam courses. This
sorting varies from school to school, and is not within the
power of central government to alter except by exhortation.
The question is how far these processes are adequate to pro-

ide stimulation, competition and companionship for clever children.

The Conservative party policy is based on the assumption that, where the cleverest 2 or 3 per cent are concerned, they are inadequate. In 1979, detailed plans were drawn up for legislation which would restore the direct grant schools in a new guise. The scheme proposed provided for means-tested grants to assist parents with the day fees at academic independent schools, provided their children passed the entrance exam. Grants were to be available to children transferring at eleven, twelve or thirteen, or at sixth-form level, depending on when the school was prepared to take them in. The Bill containing these provisions was expected to become law in the summer of 1980, allowing the scheme to begin in September 1981.

The introduction of this scheme was greeted with considerable indignation by those who represent the maintained schools. The Conservatives had come to power, pledged not only to restoring some form of direct grant but also to raising standards in comprehensives. To many it is difficult to see how standards of academic attainment can be raised in schools if the brightest children, who can set the academic pace, are removed from those schools. The controversy all but obliterated discussion of a much broader-reaching though ostensibly less dramatic suggestion. This was an idea proposed by the editor of *The Times Educational Supplement*, Stuart Maclure, in the issue of 18 April 1975.

In an attempt to find a consensus view, Mr Maclure suggested that children should follow a common course until fourteen, and then a wide range of specialization and differentiation would be allowed. Those who wanted to specialize in practical subjects and take vocational courses would be able to move on to technical schools which might be grafted on to or developed within existing further education colleges. Those with a more academic turn of mind would be grouped together on academic courses in academic schools. There would be no formal exam at fourteen, and school-leaving credentials would be made up of a series of credits from courses taken.

This scheme has attractions. It might be cheaper than all-through comprehensives, producing economics of scale by grouping expensive specialist subjects, in particular craft work or minority subjects like classics, together. Bored fifteen- and sixteen-year-olds who drain the resources of secondary schools would be offered a constructive way of escape. And for the academically inclined, it offers a compromise in the true British tradition between theoretical purity and a realistic appraisal of what is possible, a logical extension of the sorting which already goes on at fourteen. Specialist senior schools would be able to attract good specialist teachers.

Stuart Maclure's persuasive version of this policy has suffered in the attention it has received because of its similarity to Conservative policies. It has suffered in particular because, included in the original article, was the suggestion that differentiation of this sort at fourteen would provide an opportunity for integrating the independent secondary schools into the mainstream of the education service. Even without seeming to champion independent schools, the idea has snags.

Good jobs and high incomes in our society depend increasingly on educational qualifications. Any system of diversification at fourteen, however generously planned to provide for all, will produce competition for those courses which lead to academic qualifications and university places. Applications to the schools best at producing success in these terms would be bound to exceed places available. Selection, with all its well-rehearsed social drawbacks, would be inevitable, and well-established academic independent schools would gain a cachet of increased success at the expense of the maintained schools.

Furthermore, such a system would encourage specialization in arts or science or languages from fourteen. Early specialization has, as described in Chapter 4, been widely deplored and greatly reduced in recent years. Fourteen is too young to close career options by dropping crucial subjects, and too young to expect people to know which areas of study they wish particularly to develop. This applies as much to choices between practical and academic skills as it does to choices between academic subjects.

More reliable assessment of children's potential could no doubt be made at fourteen than at eleven, but if concrete decisions involving changes of school are being made at this point, the sorting process will inevitably begin well before the end of the year. This would distort any idea of all children sharing a common course on equal terms up to fourteen.

Progressive selection between eleven and fourteen would undermine the middle years of schooling still more. There could be nothing more disheartening for pupils or for the teachers teaching this age group than to have any child who showed real talent and progress transferred to another school.

The chance of children making wrong choices at fourteen must be somewhat greater than at sixteen. A scheme based on this sort of differentiation would therefore have to be backed up by an elaborate system of safeguards so that those who later regretted, for example, choosing an apprenticeship, could turn to academic study. The cost of providing the grants to make a reality of such opportunities would off-set any savings made earlier.

Perhaps the most powerful reason of all for rejecting the idea of selection between schools before sixteen is that it would involve, in almost all parts of the country, a further institutional upheaval. Many of the advantages of the scheme can be gained by careful development of courses within existing secondary schools. Most of the drawbacks apply not to differentiation of secondary courses as such but to the rigidities produced by having to decide between institutions.

Progressive selection between eleven and fourteen has received support, not only for its own supposed merits but because of the lifeline it could offer to independent schools. The underlying assumption is that the survival of separate independent schools is important because they provide an alternative to an otherwise monolithic state system.

The case for the continued existence of independent schools is beguiling. Some major pioneering work in reforming the secondary school curriculum, in particular in maths and science, has been done in independent schools. The best of the schools have staff and resources of a standard which comprehensives cannot hope to match, though the less good compare ill with the average comprehensive. The attainment of pupils at the best of these schools serves to show what young people of all abilities can master, given good teaching, the will and the opportunity.

Secondly, they provide boarding care for many who need it though not by any means for all. Most of those whose children might most profit by boarding cannot afford the fees. Many of their children are disturbed or distressed. Conditions at home through poverty or strain or both are bad and the children can be troublesome and disruptive pupils. They are most unlikely to fit into a secluded, monied atmosphere comfortably. Heads of independent boarding schools are well aware that if they took in any substantial number of such children, they would get protests from their fee-paying customers.

Thirdly, suppression of such schools would be an act of tyranny.

None the less, their continued existence is bedevilling the comprehensive enterprise. If all independent schools are to survive in the next decade while the number of school children falls by a third, they have to attract a growing proportion of the school population. In 1979 came the first signs that they are succeeding in doing this. Numbers in 1977 and 1978 had remained static, if foreign pupils were discounted. In 1979 they rose slightly, with the gain accounted for mainly by increasing numbers of girls. Over the decade 1968 to 1978, the proportion of school children in independent schools fell by nearly a fifth.

There are changes in the pattern of independent education. In April 1978, in the *Sunday Telegraph*, Dr John Rae, then chairman of the Headmaster's Conference and headmaster of Westminster School said this: 'At first it appears that despite inflation the independent schools are booming ... but a breakdown of the figures reveals a trend that could change the whole character of the independent sector.' Boys' public schools were, he said, losing boarders. Girls' schools were losing sixth formers to the boys' schools, 'making it more difficult for headmistresses to retain highly qualified staff'. Prep schools were losing eleven- to thirteen-year-olds because of competition from ex-direct grant schools. As a result, they were beginning to extend their work to O-level, and as a result were competing with weaker public schools and feeding the maintained sector after sixteen as well as the independent sector.

The aggressive marketing which this situation provokes has led the independent schools to emphasize those things which distinguish them from comprehensives: exclusivity, academic pressure, university entrance success. (Boarding seems to lack the same sales appeal these days.) Since 1977, prep schools have even taken to direct advertising.

Just as *Vogue* or *Homes and Gardens*, with their glossy consumer advertisements, influence the aspirations of those who cannot possibly either afford or indeed accommodate the products they feature, so this covert advertising by the private schools moulds parents' expectation of all schools. No similar sales job is done for the common schools. Instead, every time teachers, parents or politicians campaign for improvement in comprehensive schools, they inadvertently give credence to the careful propaganda of private schools.

A survey carried out by Tessa Bridgeman and Irene Fox, and published in *New Society* on 29 June 1978, examined people's reasons for choosing private preparatory schools. One group had had no experience of or contact with state schools. Another group would dearly have loved to use the state system but thought it was not good enough.

Ignorance or fear of the alternative are shaky foundations for the private sector. If these findings are valid, they reinforce Dr Rae's warning in his *Sunday Telegraph* article that, 'If a point is reached when middle class parents no longer feel compelled to opt out of the maintained schools, their desertion of the independent sector is likely to be sudden and wholesale rather than gradual and piecemeal.'

Such a switch would benefit the state sector most in psychological terms. If the common schools were used by the most articulate section of the population, they would gain important backing when it came to bargaining for resources and informed rather than factious criticism and pressure for improvement.

There are four possible ways of treating the independent schools other than outright abolition. The first is best summed up by Clough's couplet:

> Thou shalt not kill; but need'st not strive
> Officiously to keep alive.

As part of that policy, the remaining tax advantages which the independent schools enjoy as charities and which parents procure through life insurance endowment schemes could be removed. The way in which major companies pump funds into independent schools, both for facilities and in the form of scholarship schemes for their employees' children, could be investigated to ensure that they are not used for tax evasion purposes.

More public discussion of the way in which companies in this country have become used to rewarding their top management in kind – opera seats, Wimbledon tickets, private school fees – because they could not reward them in cash under severe incomes policies, might serve to expose the extent to which senior management in British industry is a self-perpetuating caste, educating its children separately from the children of lesser employees.

The second is to adopt a scheme like the Conservatives' assisted places scheme mentioned earlier. Removing the buffer of relatively cheap direct grant schools and free grammar schools in the 1970s had left the independent schools increasingly isolated and conspicuous as being not only unique for the affluence of their pupils but also for the selectiveness of their entry.

The assisted places scheme has been designed, as the then Conservative spokesman for education, Norman St John Stevas, said in September 1978, to 'give new hope to the bright child from a modest home'. It will cost some £55 million a year when it is fully fledged, and will, according to Conservative ministers, allow about 3 per cent of children to receive means-tested grants to help with fees. Though it is designed pri-

arily to help children not schools, it will in effect bring a
substantial chunk of public money into the independent
schools and enable them to safeguard their academic credentials in an increasingly competitive market. All past experience of academic selective schemes suggests that those who
benefit will not be the most disadvantaged, whatever efforts
are made to encourage them to apply.

A third possibility is to mesh at least some of the independent schools into the main education system as centres of
specialist work. This could be done under a scheme for differentiation at fourteen. It could also be done at sixth-form level.
There is, however, no shortage of places in state schools, and
it is not likely that this sort of scheme could make economic
sense if it simply involved removing pupils from the state
schools and sending them to independent schools on full
grants. And it would be unacceptable to introduce differential
fees – the effect of means-tested grants – in what is supposed
to be a main part of the country's provision for young people's
school education.

This possibility would therefore involve taking over a
limited number of the best independent schools. If the policy
was to select at fourteen, a few hundred young people of
exceptional brilliance in particular fields could be recruited
by national competition and gathered together at, say, Win-
chester College and a few other centres. No fee-paying pupils
would be admitted. These would simply be state schools,
mainly boarding of necessity, for a minute percentage of young
people, those whose ability was far above normal limits. Such
schools already exist for music and dancing in this country.
In the Soviet Union, about 3 per cent of children are gathered
together in this way: musicians, dancers, sportsmen and women, mathematicians, linguists, scientists. It is, however, worth
noting that the Soviet Union has ceased to set up such schools
and has now begun to look at ways of developing excellence in
these skills within ordinary schools instead.

If any idea of selection at fourteen is rejected, the alternative version of this option is to pick a limited number of
schools, but this time giving priority to those in major centres

of population. These could then be developed as academic sixth-form centres. Again, no fees would be paid. This version has been canvassed for several years with little success by John Rae. It has two major drawbacks. One is that it involves the private schools in question giving up their independence. This they are not keen to do. The other is that it would be hard to persuade people running existing comprehensive schools that they should give up all claim to cover the highest levels of academic work.

A fourth way of dealing with the independent schools is to leave them as they are and let market forces take their course.

Parents' right of choice provides the third major area in which national policy decisions will be needed. Any real element of choice has only ever existed for those who have enough brains or talent, charm or money, to make them desirable entrants to the schools they prefer. Those who failed the 11-plus and could not afford fees have had no choice but to take the school they were offered.

Two things have combined to change this to some extent. Comprehensive schools have removed the 11-plus barrier. Falling numbers of children have produced spaces in many more schools than before. What is happening now is that determination and money are becoming more important than brains in providing access to choice within the state system. Choice lies with those who know how to manipulate the system: those who can move house to be in reach of a school they like; those who gain admission to schools with good reputations by advancing passionate belief in a Christian education, in co-education or in sexual segregation, depending on the characteristics of the most esteemed local school.

In rural areas where secondary schools have large catchment areas, the problem of pecking order does not arise. In the cities it does, and decisions are needed as to how much scope for choice parents should be given. Dudley Fiske, chief education officer for Manchester, spelled out in a paper for a national conference on comprehensive schools held in York in December 1977 the consequences of allowing free parental choice in a city. One of Manchester's schools had no children with an IQ over 115 and a third with IQs below 85. At the other extreme, one had a quarter above 115 and only one in twelve below 85. Such schools are not properly comprehensives.

In Inner London, the ruling Labour group have made a degree of parental choice an important part of their platform. But, in practice, it is modified substantially by a banding system which prevents any school taking a disproportionate number of clever children or getting saddled with a disproportionate number of stupid ones. The device was, after intensive lobbying, specifically safeguarded by the 1976 Education Act (now repealed), the purpose of which was to end selection.

In many parts of the country there is less choice. Catchment areas of schools are firmly drawn and, unless parents appeal, children transfer automatically to their designated secondary school. In theory at least, this enables the authority to prevent the unequal distribution of children, and in practice, when all schools are full, it works.

But, by 1978, numbers of children were beginning to fall in secondary schools, opening up greater possibilities of choice. The weakness of the existing law became apparent. Because of loopholes in the 1944 Education Act, it was possible for determined parents to get their children into any school they wanted. For a while, a political battle threatened between those whose political support comes mainly from people who win in this sort of battle (the Conservatives) and those who are thought to champion the losers (Labour). Then pressure from both Labour and Conservative local education authorities produced a reluctant agreement from both parties at Westminster that some legislation was necessary to give local authorities power to control the numbers admitted to their schools. Such provisions were included both in the Labour Education Bill which failed to pass in the spring of 1979, and in the Bill subsequently introduced by the Conservatives in the autumn of 1979.

Without power to control admissions, the schools can be faced with large fluctuations in numbers which make planning

and staffing hard. Energetic parents can flock together so th
some schools have a high proportion of highly motivat
children. While those who get into the popular schools m
benefit, the opportunities of children left behind in less pop
lar schools are not consistent with the aims of a comprehensi
system.

The less popular schools cannot support a full range of (
level and A-level courses; they cannot attract the best teache
they tend to develop concentrations of the least tractable chi
dren; they tend to be in the least salubrious areas. The deve
opment of neighbourhood schools, reflecting the area i
which they are located, is an inevitable corollary of compr
hensive schooling. But the unrestrained development of th
pattern can be as divisive and undesirable as the old selecti
system, reinforcing patterns of class, wealth and privilege.

Falling school rolls do present a major opportunity for ir
provement in the state system. The question is whether
allow all the benefit to accrue to the strong by letting fr
choice have as long a rein as possible; or whether to restrai
that choice in order to use the slack in schools to upgrade th
whole system, closing bad schools and moving children out
run-down buildings, reducing class sizes all round and ensu
ing that all children have access to a full range of scho
courses.

Clever children will be much affected by the development ov
the next few years of the public exam system. Although th
rhetoric is all about the need for exams to follow the cu
riculum rather than dictate what is taught, in practice th
terminal exams at sixteen and at eighteen are the only wa
in which the British education system is at present measure
and controlled nationally.

The Labour government decided in the autumn of 197
to adopt the proposals, submitted to it by the Schools Counc
and re-examined in detail by a special study group under Si
James Waddell, for combining O-level and CSE into a singl
system of 16-plus exams, the General Certificate of Secondar
Education. Most subjects should, it was suggested, be exam

ed by a series of papers, some taken by all candidates but me designed specially for the more advanced and some for e slower. The highest grades, deliberately pegged to the ass standards for O-level, would be given only to those who ass the harder papers. In 1979, the Conservatives postponed definitely decisions on the introduction of the new exams, ereby pushing back the first possible date for their introduc- on beyond 1986.

The new system has obvious merits in ironing out adminis- ative complications, duplication and invidious distinctions ising from the present dual system. But it has the disadvant- e of making it rather easier than it had been to leave open ecisions about who should take which exams until nearer e exam itself. At present the decision can only be postponed eyond the beginning of the fourth year in schools which have eir own purpose-built mode 3 CSEs meshing very closely ith O-level syllabuses. The new exams would sharpen the ntral dilemma: postponing decisions is good for those who atch up late: it is bad for those who are slowed down by wait- g. The new exams could make it easier to carry on with asses of wide ability until at least the end of the fourth year hen children are fifteen, particularly in rather small schools hich could then offer more options. This could mean that e clever will get relatively little, perhaps two or three rms, teaching in homogeneous groups before they take their xams. It could also mean that clever children are tempted opt for an easier set of papers when they could not have stified choosing CSE instead of O-level. The new system ould require even greater vigilance by teachers to prevent oung people coasting along. It would involve an even greater sk of lazy pupils and teachers working to the norm rather an reaching for the limits. Wide ability groups are generally cknowledged to become harder to teach successfully as chil- ren get older. There is no reason why the new exams should ecessarily make such groups more common, but there is very ground for supposing they might. And, for the clever, hat would not be a good thing, unless they have very good and ell-supported teachers.

Unless the new exams are seen to be designed in such way as to ensure that the bright are stretched – and M Shirley Williams was most insistent, both in person and in th White Paper describing the proposed changes, that they mu be – they will not inspire much confidence or do anything allay public worries about comprehensive schools.

By mid 1979, the GCE boards were deeply involved working out details for administering the new exams. The participation will be crucial to success and will probably e sure that the reform comes about by gradual steps even the government does nothing. Further behind in the pip line are proposals to reform 18-plus exams. A-level has lon been under attack as too narrow, confining clever youn people from sixteen onwards to three main subjects. Less cleve pupils may take only one or two subjects.

Since 1964, proposals for reform have been under di cussion by the Schools Council, the government's offici advisory body on school curricula and examinations. The u shot after many vicissitudes was the proposal that A-level b replaced by Normal (N-) and Further (F-) level exams. Brigh children – three A-level candidates – would take five subject three at N-level and two at F-level, and this, it was suggeste should be the standard qualification for higher education.

A broad sixth-form course has great attractions and is muc more consistent with comprehensive schooling than is nar row specialization. Making the exams for eighteen-year-old into a broad test of general education would help to under line their function as the terminal school exams. At presen their structure and content is, to a large extent, dictated b the demands of the universities. Only about half of all A-leve candidates go on to higher education, while the others g into a variety of jobs and other training courses. A five- or six subject exam more in line with the French or internationa *baccalaureats* or the German *Abitur* would be more appro priate. What the institutions of higher education make o young people who then seek to go on studying becomes separate issue.

It is difficult to detach A-level from the universities, sinc the exam is controlled by exam boards which themselves owe their existence to universities. There is no equivalent voice which can speak for employers, parents or students who might want to argue for a broader sixth-form course. The N or F scheme was a compromise. The F-level tier exams were designed entirely to satisfy the universities that students coming to them would still have a sufficient grounding in their subject to make a three-year honours degree course possible without lowering standards. As such it failed to satisfy them, and, on top of that, the complications of the scheme produced an unequivocal rejection, even from those who favoured a broader sixth-form curriculum.

Instead, support seemed in 1979 to be growing for a suggestion made by Mr Ian Beer, headmaster of Lancing, to the Headmasters' Conference in 1978. Mr Beer proposed that A-level be kept and N-level introduced as soon as possible (as half an A-level) on its own. This relatively simple scheme would be capable of almost immediate introduction and would allow students a choice between breadth and specialization. In 1979, the GCE boards declared to the education secretary their willingness to go ahead with such an intermediate exam. The idea appears to have the backing of the universities – a crucial factor in any change if only because their opposition causes inordinate delay. Some faculties would continue, as now, to demand a high degree of specialization in the form of particular groups of A-levels, but others might willingly accept, for example, two A-levels and two N-levels as an alternative.

Such exams could be linked with another suggestion, also made in the autumn of 1978 by Dr Harry Judge in *The Times Educational Supplement* (27 October). This was that the Secretary of State introduce a Diploma of General Education for eighteen-year-olds. People would qualify for it by clocking up a number of units based on a wide range of qualifications – A-levels, N-levels, O-levels, CSEs, even technician qualifications. The diploma would then become the basic qualification for higher education and mandatory student grants, replacing the present two A-levels. It would be open to the government to vary the requirements for receipt of the diploma. They could require some maths and English passes at some specified level. They could build in a breadth requirement, thereby forcing students and universities into accepting a wider sixth form curriculum. This, too, could be introduced without delay.

Higher education is now the only part of the education service solely concerned with cleverer pupils. Decisions about its future uniquely affect them.

A major challenge is facing higher education, one wider than that of reacting constructively to changes in schools. Allegations that there is too much academic isolation in British higher education and too little willingness to look dispassionately at the industrial needs of the nation have been loud in recent years. So have complaints from comprehensive school teachers that this country's most prestigious universities are unwilling to accept that clever young people are not attracted by their elegant patrician ways. Oxford and Cambridge tutors are accused of preferring the well-trained products of traditional schools run by old friends to the more diverse and less disciplined talents of children who have pursued academic work for its own sake against the majority, or who combine academic with practical skills.

The universities have sound arguments on their side. If this country is going to continue to turn out graduates of internationally recognized standard after only three years, unlike any other country, universities have to insist on a high level of preparation being done by the schools. Claims that A-level courses now embrace what used to be first-year university work are evidence that the schools are increasingly being required to join directly in the enterprise of maintaining the standard of the three-year British undergraduate degree.

It may not be desirable to do this indefinitely. In the 1980s numbers will begin to fall in higher education and it will be possible to expand many degree courses to four years without extra cost. There is likely to be a strong lobby for doing so: those who shout loudest about low standards now could be the first to fall victim to retrenchments later. Some of the east popular universities have been the source of some of the loudest criticisms of schools.

Already the three-year degree is under pressure, despite the continued existence of A-levels. Southampton University is one of eight universities which have introduced a four-year engineering degree. The reason is not that standards have fallen but that the three-year degree was not proving an adequate qualification in a competitive European market compared with much longer continental courses. The extra year will be offered only to the best students and will add a design and management component to their training.

People like Sir Alex Smith at Manchester Polytechnic, and Dr Patrick Nuttgens at Leeds Polytechnic, have been shouting the gospel of a broader range of values for many years. In the universities, rare people like Lord Bullock, Master of St Catherine's College, Oxford, have seen clearly the need to break the tight grip of academic values on the secondary school system. But, by and large, the universities have not responded with speed or enthusiasm. They could relinquish or loosen their grip on school exams. They could improve the practical and applied content of their courses, but with the exception of the technological universities, like those at Bath and Loughborough, they have not done so. They could alternatively retire to train academics in more limited numbers. They have not done this either.

Despite government attempts to limit university numbers in order to protect the polytechnics and colleges with their supposed practical bias, universities have grown at the expense of local authority controlled institutions. If this trend continues, they could be taking an increasing proportion of all students in the next decade and could use their popularity to avoid changing their ways. Already they get the best students and their students get the best jobs. What they offer are mostly highly academic courses. If it is true that academic values have been over-emphasized in British education, this circle needs in some way to be broken, either by the universities themselves or by outside action designed to improve the esteem of alternative forms of advanced education and training.

127

It may be students who will force the change. At Bath University in recent years, entrants to applied science and technology courses have had a steadily rising standard of A-level passes.

University subjects which yield marketable qualifications have been moving up in popularity since the mid 1970s. This is a more promising development than the rather tentative attempts made by the previous Labour government to plan for the future structure of higher education. In two papers, *Higher Education into the 1990s* (1978) and *Future Trends in Higher Education* (1979), the population figures and figures showing the proportion of eighteen-year-olds going on to full-time study were dutifully set out. Suggestions were made for coping with an expected increase in numbers until the mid 1980s, and then with a sustained contraction. The whole exercise was highly theoretical, concentrating on guesses about young people's future intentions without ever discussing the effect that government policy could have on these.

Numbers going on to higher education of various kinds could be greatly affected by government grants policy. At present this does not encourage students to take practical and technical courses outside universities to the same extent as it does academic courses. It does not encourage employers to release staff for long courses of advanced study. It does not make it practically possible for people who dropped out of school at sixteen to return to full-time study.

Quick visits to a few universities and polytechnics do much to explain why universities get the pick of students. Staff calibre apart, buildings are of better quality and better cleaned. There is more and better accommodation for students. There is also a central clearing house for admissions so that there is no need to try one institution after another in search of a place on a suitable course. These things will need to be rectified if polytechnics and colleges are to compete successfully with universities.

The Education Bill which was lost in 1979 contained provision for a central body to manage the local authority controlled side of higher education. This could in time have led o the establishment of a central clearing house for places in polytechnics and colleges. Its main purpose, however, was to produce more efficient management of funding. That rationalization was indefinitely delayed by the change of government in 1979. At the same time, the polytechnics and colleges, like the schools, suffered severely from local authority spending cuts. While the universities did not escape, central coordination by the University Grants Committee helped to ensure that cuts were made in an orderly way. By contrast, each polytechnic and college was subject to the whims of its particular local authority as well as the government imposing a limit on the total spent by this section.

The burden of bridging the gap between school and higher education is borne to a large extent by sixth forms: the transit camps in the present system between mass schools and élite higher education. Their short- and long-term future is the most important organizational question now facing the school system.

The debate which rages over sixth forms is intricate and acrimonious, with administrative, economic and educational threads all tangled up with strong vested interests. In 1977, the Department of Education drew up and circulated privately for discussion a paper which suggested that as many as four out of five comprehensive sixth forms were not viable. This calculation was based on the assumption that staffing ratios in sixth forms should not be more generous than 1 : 10, and that a genuinely comprehensive education service should not reduce to less than sixteen the number of subjects at A-level offered to sixth formers. This gave then a working minimum for viable sixth forms of a hundred A-level students.

On this basis, many comprehensive sixth forms were too small and offered too few subjects, and though things might get better in the short term, as numbers began to fall in the 1980s things would get worse. The department therefore proposed to ask local authorities to consider coordinating and bringing together their sixth-form work.

The suggestion was greeted with outraged indignation, particularly by head teachers. The department therefore shelved the matter, preferring to include discussions of sixth forms in a White Paper covering all provision for sixteen- to nineteen-year-olds which was to have been published in 1979.

Behind the decision to press for some concentrations of sixth-form work lay an unstated belief that academic standards in comprehensive schools were in danger. Publicly, expansion of opportunity was the reason given. It was argued that a good range of A-level subjects should be offered to all sixth formers; that clever children should be gathered together in sufficient numbers to provide competition and companionship; that groups of under about five students were too expensive to staff.

The head of School D, recently reorganized, made the case: 'Last year [the last year in which this school had a grammar school sixth form] there were sixteen pupils doing A-level biology. Fourteen of them went to university, three to Oxford or Cambridge. Of the others, one went into nursing, the other to a polytechnic to read pharmacy. They were working with first-class people. Now, with a group the same size but with a wider spread, they do not get the environment and competition and then staff expectations begin to go down.'

Sixth-form college, School R, with 800 pupils had eight A-level English groups, averaging about thirteen in each. They had been able to stream them, and as a result the pace of the top two groups had picked up to what the staff described as first-year university standard. They were also bringing together potential Oxford and Cambridge candidates from the beginning of the second sixth-form year so that the best 5 to 10 per cent of the college's intake would have extra work timetabled. In previous years, until the seventh term, it was done 'in cupboards and at lunch time'.

Already this college sent about twenty students to Oxford and Cambridge every year, and hoped to send more. Like others, it showed encouraging results, and it was not surprising that administrators and parents saw here a possible solution to their problems with bright children. Indeed, in some areas the sixth-form colleges are reserved specifically for the bright. There were half a dozen in 1977 which only admitted A-level students.

Sixth-form colleges – all of them, but conspicuously the more selective and deliberately academic of them – are being welcomed with open arms by admissions tutors at Oxford and Cambridge universities, who see here a politically less sensitive source of supply than the independent and direct grant schools, yet one with which they can build the same sort of close personal relations and from which they can expect students with high levels at academic preparation.

Some of the colleges adopt a deliberately open policy, turning their backs on what they regard as academic snobbery and cramming in favour of more radical ways. They have been pioneers of the engineering technology and applied physics A-levels. And they have accused universities of under-valuing this sort of qualification: accusations which have been hotly denied by technological universities, but conspicuously not by the old, academic ivory towers.

The sixth-form college should in fact be able to do both jobs economically. Thirty-four local authorities have now settled for some sort of separate provision after sixteen in at least some part of their bailiwicks. In 1979, there were eighty-eight sixth-form colleges. There were another fourteen tertiary colleges – that is, colleges which include further education and adult courses as well as the usual school courses. And the numbers are growing.

The difference between sixth-form and tertiary colleges turns mainly on whether the colleges are run as schools or as colleges of further education. This affects the scales of pay, and, in practice, the union affiliation of those who teach in the college, whether school teachers or further education teachers. It also affects the courses that can be offered. Schools seldom teach vocational courses, because they lack qualified staff and specialized equipment.

The tertiary college, though rarer because administratively more difficult to organize, has more attractions than the sixth-form college since it embraces a wider population both in age and interests. It enables people to combine courses across academic and vocational demarcation lines. It offers the possibility of part-time and full-time study at a wide range of levels to people throughout their lives.

Tertiary colleges are likely to become more common when the conflicting sets of regulations governing them are standardized. As numbers fall, local authorities will be strongly tempted to concentrate at least minority subject sixth-form teaching in their further education colleges. The colleges would probably be most unwilling not to offer the main subjects as well, and wholesale transfer of sixth-form work could increase. The proportion of university entrants coming from further education colleges is already rising and must include many who moved to further education because they were disenchanted with school, whether state or private.

The development of open-access tertiary colleges represents the extension of the comprehensive principle of education to the whole of the population over sixteen. And even below sixteen, links are being forged. When the school-leaving age was raised to sixteen in 1973–4, many schools and colleges got together to organize building, catering, motor maintenance and similar courses for those compelled to stay on. In 1978, tentative soundings were made by the Engineering Industry Training Board for a scheme allowing young people to begin work on apprentice courses in their last two years at school. This would allow young people to work in a college while remaining on their school's register. The idea was not generally well received.

At the more academic levels, the links between schools and further education are harder to develop. While schools are happy to lose their less able and perhaps bored pupils, they often cling tenaciously to the brighter. In the first place, in most areas it makes a substantial difference to the school. Allowances for books, materials and staff are more generous for sixth formers, and the number of senior posts in schools depends on the number of children of each age: the higher the proportion of older children the greater the number of teachers the school can promote.

There is every bureaucratic incentive for the schools to

hold on to sixth formers. There are also educational incentives. Removing sixth-form pupils, and with them advanced-level teaching from secondary schools, is the major drawback to sixth-form and tertiary colleges. It removes a source of professional satisfaction from the teachers. It removes what one head described as 'the vision of excellence' from the younger children. And, for the able, it makes impossible what another head described as essential: seeing the whole period from the fourth to the seventh year as one piece and tailoring courses accordingly. It removes from schools like School J the certainty that they can compensate in the sixth form for any losses in the fourth and fifth years. But, most important of all, to quote the head of School S, who had seen her school change from a highly regarded girls' grammar school to a mixed eleven to sixteen school, 'I get less staff with first-class degrees than I used to and there are a decreasing number in the school who have had any experience of high-powered post-O-level teaching. I am very conscious of the level the top lot can reach, but some of my staff are not.

Girls, now at six-form college, School R, who were in School S during the time it changed, noticed that, in their time there, the pressure of work, the academic content and standards applied to their homework and to their habits generally diminished; though one girl, who moved into the school half-way through from a comprehensive in Wales, found it by contrast remarkably tough.

Largely forgotten in the course of the debate about sixth forms is research which Professor Eric Hoyle carried out with Mr T. Christie for the Public Schools Commission (already mentioned on page 68). Their aim was to test the theory that able children do best if they are grouped together to form 'a critical mass'. First, five élite schools, direct grant and grammar, in the north of England were chosen for having the best O-level results with the Joint Matriculation Board. Their A-level results two years later were then checked to see if the schools' superiority, compared to other schools, was sustained. It was not.

Secondly, Hoyle and Christie carried out a complicated

comparison of the performance of those doing best and those doing worst at O-level and at A-level in the five schools and in ninety-four other schools. They found that fewer boys (they were all boys' schools) did well at A-level than had done at O-level in the élite schools. This was not so in the other schools.

In a booklet, *Gifted Children and Their Education*, which Professor Hoyle and Dr J. Wilks wrote in 1974 for the Department of Education, they say of these findings that they:

Do not support the view that bringing together very bright children under one roof improves their general level of attainment – at least where A-level is a criterion. One might indeed very tentatively draw the opposite conclusion. One very tentative hypothesis is that even in the highly selective school a stratification of pupils, either officially through streaming or unofficially through the informal pupil culture, inhibits the achievements of those lower in the hierarchy.

The same pamphlet also reports further studies made by Hoyle and Wilks in Manchester which showed that, where schools had express streams to O-level, numbers going to university were proportionately lower than in schools with no express stream.

Two sixth formers in a comprehensive school unwittingly – and unscientifically – gave support to Professor Hoyle's hypothesis. 'Here they cosset us 'cos we're rare birds. At the grammar school [the local one, now independent] you'd be one of so many that unless you were outstanding they wouldn't really bother.' But then they had just had a bad time at the hands of the grammar school. Their own school, School J, teaches no Latin and they wanted to learn it. It was arranged they should join in the other school's crash course for beginners. 'They looked at us as if we were some kind of freaks. "You do have O-levels, don't you?" they said. They behave as if an O-level from a comprehensive is somehow less good.' The arrangement unsurprisingly petered out.

The sixth-form college, School R, which set such store by academic English teaching (described in Chapter 2, pages 58–9) may be having the same effect. One of those English teachers who was so enthusiastic about the effects of A-level streaming had been charged by the principal with studying the progress of both the most and the least able. With the most able, he correlated O-level results when they arrived with their subsequent A-level grades. This had led him to the conclusion that, 'Those with C at O-level have virtually no chance of getting A to C at A-level, anyway in the major subjects.' The principal, though apparently not the teacher, was acutely aware of the danger of self-fulfilling prophecy.

All of these factors form part of the current debate about the future of post-sixteen education. The debate is bitter because more structural reorganization would be involved in changing to sixth-form or tertiary colleges, and people are, after a decade of disruption, understandably wary of that even if they are not against the idea in principle.

The quality of what is done in schools depends most of all upon the quality of the teachers and the leadership of the head teacher. Two pieces of research published in the late 1970s have revealed the extent to which schools themselves make a difference to children's success. This has always been obvious to parents. It has too seldom been accepted by comprehensive school teachers.

David Reynolds published an article in *New Society* on 29 July 1976, called 'Schools Do Make a Difference'. In it he set out findings from a study carried out in Welsh schools. Academic attainment, rates of delinquency, truanting and the chances of getting a job all varied markedly from school to school, even when the children came from similar backgrounds and had similar ability. Furthermore, these characteristics marched together: low truancy, high attainment, low delinquency, low unemployment.

Michael Rutter, professor of child psychiatry at London University, published a much larger study along the same lines in 1979. *Fifteen Thousand Hours* is an account of many years' research. London school children in a group of comprehensives in a deprived part of the city were followed through from primary school to sixteen. Twelve comprehensives were studied in detail. The results showed the same sort of pattern as did David Reynolds's, but went further, identifying the particular characteristics of schools which seemed most to influence children's success.

Streaming, severe discipline and caning, the size of schools, the amount of money they had to spend and the social class background of the children did not apparently affect results. What did make a difference was a friendly and encouraging atmosphere; a clean and attractively decorated building with comfortable places for children to work; and teachers who had high expectations of their pupils, who were readily accessible at any time to talk over problems, who dealt with disruption quietly and calmly and who prepared their lessons and came to class on time. It was also important that the school had a reasonable number of bright children. Where there were few, standards of attainment were lower for all. Where there were enough bright children, it was noticeable that schools which did well for these children were the same ones which did well for all their pupils, both in terms of academic achievement and in terms of behaviour.

This study is of major importance, one of the most valuable guides to improving standards in schools. It does not suggest radical reorganization or vast expenditure. It does suggest that remedies lie in the hands of existing staff. There is little which national governments can do to force this sort of improvement upon schools. Confidence will be the most important factor in producing change. All the same, there are some things which can be done to help local authorities to guide and manage the work of their schools.

The first concerns management of the teaching force. One of the drawbacks to stability is that the best young people emerging from teacher training find it hard to get jobs, while there are in schools some teachers who were hired when staff were hard to get. Not all of them were good.

Provision has been made to allow local authorities to offer early retirement at fifty with an enhanced pension to people whose departure is conducive to 'the efficient function of the service'. There are growing signs that this will be a favourite way of dealing with congestion. It will not be cheap, but it is humane and effective; much more effective than trying to up-grade rather dreary middle-aged teachers by sending them on in-service training courses.

No similarly elegant way has been found of persuading in-effective teachers in their twenties and thirties to leave. More generous arrangements for retraining for other jobs might help. More careful staff management by head teachers and education officers might lead to more teachers deciding to try their fortune in other fields. In time, accumulating case law from industrial tribunals may establish a pattern for sacking any who are seriously incompetent.

A productivity deal with teachers could radically affect the conduct of schools by making it easier for local authorities and head teachers to insist on reasonable standards. Negotiating machinery was set up at the end of 1978 by local authorities to discuss teachers' conditions of service. Talks were held in parallel with pay negotiations, but for statutory reasons agreements cannot be made part of pay settlements. Legislation may be necessary to remove this division.

In the course of negotiations about conditions of service, a suggestion made in a government Green Paper, *Education in Schools* (1977), should be examined. The idea, so well buried that it received little attention, was that machinery should be set up by each education authority regularly to assess the performance of all their teachers. With regular reports available, authorities would be able to call to account those who were not satisfactory.

Teachers' contracts also need examination. These are at present vague. By custom and practice they can be said to in-clude an obligation to do an unspecified amount of work on top of taking lessons. Marking books, attending staff meetings, talking to parents, preparing lessons would come high on the list of duties teachers are expected to perform. Running clubs, helping with school outings, attending parent-teacher associa-tion meetings might come rather lower. The extent of the obligation is uncertain, and the differences between teachers in the amount of time they devote to such things is remarkable.

If in exchange for more money – for example, bringing

teachers' pay back in real terms to the level secured as a result of the Houghton Report in 1974 – teachers agreed to a standard contract which specified their obligations outside as well as inside classrooms, local authorities would have some control. They would have some assurance that more money and improved pupil–teacher ratios will not simply mean that lazy teachers do less work, while energetic ones, as before, are left to carry too heavy a load.

The success of schemes of this kind will depend to a large extent on money, for the second way in which central government can help the local authorities improve the service is with money. If major improvements are to be procured, savings should not be made on the national education budget as the school population shrinks. Money is not of itself the most important thing in improving standards in schools, as Michael Rutter showed (see page 135), but it helps. Parsimony breeds bitterness which is not conducive to general goodwill and co-operation.

Smaller age groups, children born after the mid 1960s, are coming through the schools, behind unprecedented large groups born in the earlier 1960s. Older children are more expensive to educate. Staffing, allowances for books and equipment all go up as children get older. The *per capita* cost of a primary school child in 1978–9 was £337, of a secondary child £505, of a university student nearly £2,500 (though this figure is differently calculated). Not until the mid 1990s will the bulge clear full-time education altogether.

There is speculation that by then the birthrate will have risen again. There was an up-turn in 1978 which was sustained into 1979. Crystal-ball gazing is notoriously unreliable, but the best policy now must be to contract the system in such a way that later expansion is possible without serious dislocation.

To do this, local authorities – as argued earlier – need their hands strengthened in managing decline, and they need money. As numbers fall, economies of scale are lost. More teachers are needed per head, and more heating, lighting, libraries and so forth. If the money is available, declining numbers should provide the opportunity to reduce the difficulty of the school's and teacher's job: more time to prepare and mark work, more time to retrain people, more time to look after new teachers, smaller classes. It would be possible to do these things progressively over the years if spending were held level in real terms. Unfortunately, there is no prospect of any such policy. In 1979–80, local government spending was summarily cut by 3 per cent with further and larger cuts planned for subsequent years.

The sorts of things which suffer first when spending on education is cut are books, extra part-time teachers, music teaching, craft materials, extra teachers on the staff of a primary school, foreign language assistants in secondary schools. These are the things which make the difference between a school being able or not able to organize enrichment groups in maths or Latin. Second foreign languages are particularly vulnerable, so are musical instrument teaching and the enormously expensive craft technology courses.

For able children, life in a comprehensive is greatly affected by the existence of such groups and facilities, and cuts can be inordinately damaging. In the end, faced with a stark choice, most schools will feel they must give priority to non-readers rather than Latin groups and to mainstream English teaching rather than social studies A-level for three people.

The view is rapidly gaining ground that the solution to the dilemmas facing schools is not streaming in the early years nor doctrinaire imposition of mixed ability grouping. It is the endless pursuit of a reasonable balance of interests: a time-consuming, exhausting business, requiring constant fine tuning, shifting groups, individual care, detailed monitoring. Only in this way, it is argued, is it possible to bring children up without crushing the spirits of any of them – clever or stupid.

It is much harder to foster the individual talents of a class of thirty-five than of a class of eighteen. It takes longer to mark homework for thirty-five than for eighteen. For eighteen it may be possible to set different tasks and discuss work individually, to guide their reading, encourage their interests. For thirty-five there can be little chance.

It is certainly simpler to stream a school once and for all
than it is to operate a system of flexible teaching groups which
shift and change as talents emerge and develop. A shifting
pattern requires constant monitoring lest children chop and
change too much and end up not learning much. Where in
streamed schools it is only the borderline cases who have to
be agonized over, in a more flexible set-up every child becomes
borderline in some respect. Running such a system is bound
to be more expensive of time, and teachers' time is limited.
The only way to increase it is to hire more staff.

No formal recognition has ever been made that comprehensive schooling, if it is to work properly, is bound to be more
expensive than selective schooling. There is now every prospect that schools will be required to attempt the job on ever-
diminishing funds. There is every prospect, too, that when
expectations over standards are not met, the schools and not
the government's economic strategy will be blamed.

mmense excitement and energy were expended during the
970s, both in coping with the manifest difficulties of establish-
ng a comprehensive school system and in pioneering new
trategies appropriate to it. Now that some degree of stability
s returning to schools, there is a recognition that, in the pro-
ess, straight academic, traditional schooling for clever children has been to some degree neglected. Recognition is more
often tacit than explicit, comprehensive teachers have become wary of giving hostages to fortune in an unfriendly
world. But, for all that, there is now widespread agreement
that it was a mistake to suppose the bright could look after
themselves. (Their parents have too often looked after them
by taking them away to private schools.) There is a growing
realization that these children are no different from any others.
They must be pushed. They are not all marvellously self-
motivating. They will not of their own will undertake the
hard slog required to master tough subjects. Teachers in
comprehensive schools, some of whom may have had little contact with clever children or their parents before, are increasingly aware that it is no good blandly assuring parents that
there is, 'No need to worry. She's doing fine. Well above average.'

There are serious disagreements in the teaching profession
and among administrators about how loafing can be remedied
without losing the gains associated with ending selection and
postponing categorization. It is right that there should be
debate since there are no simple or clear solutions, and there
are signs everywhere that the matter is now receiving attention.

During the years of compulsory schooling, the least able
children may get priority, but the balance is redressed for
clever children in the sixth form, when the conscripts are

gone. Well over half of all state schools now have sixth forms where only one in five had them before comprehensive reorganization. When small sixth-form classes are added to the equation of advantage, the apparent favouring of the least able in terms of the schools' resources, noticeable in many schools in the early secondary years, vanishes.

School D, whose timetable showed so favourable a distribution of resources to the least able at thirteen (page 23) had A-level pupils in classes which averaged around ten, a figure which masked ones and twos for second modern languages, four for music and thirteen to sixteen in science groups. It also timetabled three periods a week for each department, during which they could do extra work with potential Oxford and Cambridge candidates during their fourth term in the sixth form.

School A, which enjoyed a reputation good enough to bolster house prices in its pleasant area by several hundred pounds, had a remarkably relaxed attitude to homework and mixed ability teaching in the first two years. 'I'd rather eleven-to-thirteen-year-olds had a broad, lively, interesting education with time to do other things like play chess or go fishing. They do just as well when they come out. As a language teacher, I find that when they are settled and expected to knuckle down in the third year, they go remarkably fast. A great deal of what the grammar schools do in the first three years is not necessary. It is quite possible to get through without,' the head said.

He rested his confidence on the sixth form and was critical of the value of what he regarded as punitive and pointless cramming of younger children in grammar and independent schools. Entry to the sixth was a privilege, and, to remain in it, hard work and plenty of it were required.

Half the children stayed on, making a sixth form of over 200, three quarters of them studying for A-level. In 1976 all candidates in ten of the fourteen subjects offered passed, and only one failed in each of the other four. The school took in twenty or more new pupils to its sixth form each year, some of them filched from fee-paying schools.

The exam figures looked somewhat better than they really
ere since not all those who embarked on A-level courses in
e end sat the exam. Even so, some three quarters of those
ho started a course passed, and that was above the national
verage of 70 per cent. The school was quite prepared to keep
eople on for a seventh term in the sixth form and to coach
em for Oxford and Cambridge entrance; and the head was
uite prepared to use personal contacts to help get them in.

In the long term, it is uncertain whether schools – particu-
rly smaller ones – will be able to hold on to their sixth
orms. (The issues surrounding this vexed question were dis-
ussed in Chapter 5, pages 129–35.) In the short term, many
uthorities are shying away from radical action for the time
eing because they want to give their schools a period of
ability after the years of upheaval. They also want to keep
e high-powered teachers and specialist approach in lower
econdary schools while they go through the process of re-
ppraising what they do for bright children. 'We must hoick
p the standards in the secondary schools first,' is the argu-
ent of London's Education Officer, Peter Newsam. It is
choed all over the country.

Instead of drastic surgery, a number of less dramatic
trategies are being tried in the hope of giving clever chil-
ren more stimulating work and company, showing teachers
hat can be done, and cutting costs a bit.

There are a variety of consortia arrangements where schools
re grouped together to share sixth-form work. The most far-
eaching of these is in Birmingham. It has not, despite strenu-
us efforts, been particularly successful. There is a great deal
f jealously, and there is a marked tendency for children to
hoose subjects which their own schools happen to offer. For
ll the difficulties, Birmingham's consortia arrangements are
ow being extended to embrace some O-level work in minority
ubjects as well. Here the chances of success look even bleaker.

While the logic of such schemes is clear, the practical snags
are many. Schools do not lightly give up their advanced teaching in a subject, because they know that they then run the risk
of losing not only the best teachers but also the best academic

pupils who gravitate at eleven to schools which offer high powered courses. If advanced work is spread out, one subject in this school, one in another, the children can spend too much time trailing around.

In Oxfordshire, a grand consortium scheme for a centre for advanced education collapsed in all but name for lack of any central leadership. No one was able to overrule the competing vested interests and loyalties of the five institutions: four schools and the West Oxfordshire Technical College. Pupils tended either to leave school and go to the college or to confine their subject choices to those available in their own school.

In Coventry, the education authority explained the advantages of cooperation and left to the schools the responsibility for making their own arrangements. In music, this seems to have worked to a limited extent on an informal basis, but in the academic subjects little had happened.

In Leeds, plans for groups of schools to share sixth-form teaching in subjects which do not attract large numbers of students had not been realized. Long meetings and intricate planning on paper produced few tangible results. The best which education officials were able to say in 1979, after all their efforts was that, 'We hope we have done the groundwork so that when smaller age groups reach the sixth forms, quick action will be possible.'

Inner London's arrangements take more account of vested interests. Consortia arrangements work fairly well in the rare cases where two neighbouring schools agree to pool their sixth forms, draw up a common timetable and share all the teaching. Cooperation soon reaches tentacles down into the fourth- and fifth-year courses since there are evident advantages in all sixth formers having had the same preparation.

Arrangements where more schools are involved and they are further apart work less well. Common timetabling and shared resources become impossible and schools resent vague exhortations to 'get together'. In recognition of this, in areas of the city where sixth forms are sparse, the Inner London Educational Authority (ILEA) has set up two sixth-form centres one in Tower Hamlets and one in Islington. Teachers and pupils from local schools forgather there for A-level work, but remain on the roll of their own schools. The centres depend heavily on good transport, and the cooperation of heads of a large number of schools, all close by and none with a large academic sixth form.

Inner London has also been experimenting with one- and two-week crash courses for older pupils – mainly A-level students, but occasionally very bright younger pupils – in the holidays and in the dog days of the summer term when exams are over. In 1978, twenty-seven subjects were taken by over 1,600 students. Sixth formers are selected by their schools, and schools with small groups and less A-level expertise get preference over the large, long-established sixth forms. The idea is that the real high fliers should be given a chance to work with their peers and with the best teachers the authority can muster from its own schools or borrow from outside. In practice, some schools have chosen to send along their marginal candidates in the hope of raising them over the A-level threshold. This was not the original intention of the courses, the range of which includes biology at St Thomas's Hospital and art at the National Gallery.

Total immersion language courses have been particularly successful. South Bank Polytechnic in London has been one of the pioneers, but much of the work on this method of teaching languages has been done at York University under the supervision of Professor Eric Hawkins. Dr Trudi Berger, who teaches York's student language teachers Italian to O-level in a fortnight, is their star exponent of the method.

York University's Language Teaching Centre has – along with others – been working on new language proficiency exams which could radically alter traditional language examining. These, like music or dancing exams, go in graded steps from below the equivalent of CSE to above A-level. They are not intended to be taken at any specific age. London, Northumberland, Edinburgh, Hertfordshire, Oxfordshire and North Yorkshire are all experimenting with these schemes.

With modern languages other than French evidently losing

the battle for a major place in the regular school timetable against the competition of sciences and craft subjects, developments of this kind are greeted with optimism. School language teaching in Britain has never been successful in producing competent speakers, and on the university side they would probably welcome anything which rescued minority languages from their present parlous state. Universities have become accustomed to accepting people to read classics who have done no Greek, though they do sometimes require attendance at one of the classics summer schools. The same will increasingly happen with other languages.

The Joint Association of Classical Teachers' summer school in ancient Greek has been running now for eleven years. It is closely associated with the Cambridge classics courses. These courses have transformed the teaching of Latin, and more recently Greek, to beginners, in the process saving them from threatened oblivion. A similar summer school – though not residential – now forms part of the ILEA programme.

Attempts are also being made by local authorities to open up for their comprehensive school students the rather forbidding path to Oxford and Cambridge. They have found support in the universities from people worried at the preponderance of independent school pupils among their entrants. In 1978, half a dozen Oxford colleges agreed to offer places to science students from London comprehensives, regardless of the grades they might get at A-level. The pupils were picked out by their teachers and the ILEA's science advisors as having great potential which they had failed fully to develop because of the limited science teaching in their schools. The colleges decreed that, if A-level grades did fall far short of the levels usually required, the students would be given some coaching before they entered the university to bring them up to standard. The progress of these students will be carefully monitored. Part of the colleges' interest in the scheme is to check how well their normal entry procedures identify very clever young people who have been badly taught. They also want to see how easily such students catch up.

It is not simply at the sixth-form and university entrance

evel that local authorities are now turning their attention
o the quality as opposed to the structure of the education
ervice. Many authorities have central arrangements for music,
nd run their own youth orchestras, and the amount of
ctivity has been steadily increasing since counties like Leices-
ershire, one of the early pioneers both of comprehensives and
f school music, showed the way.

In Inner London, curricular guidelines for school music
vere issued by the authority in 1978 to help teachers 'extend
he ways in which pupils respond to music and to encourage
ensitivity when listening, performing and inventing'. And a
elevision programme on London school music in 1977 demon-
trated the remarkable work that can be done in music and
drama, given imaginative teaching. Such work is being developed by the Schools Council project, 'Music in the Secondary School Curriculum', based at York University.

Some authorities make central provision for drama and for
ports. In Leeds, four drama teachers are appointed to senior
obs in large secondary schools with a specific responsibility for
developing drama for young people in the whole area around
he school. Anyone over thirteen can go to evening and Satur-
day sessions.

The Leeds Athletics Institutes, one in each of the five divisions of the authority, have long catered for children with
particular skills and enthusiasms in sports. In 1978, first sound-
ngs were being made to extend the principle of central provision to academic subjects. The authority hoped to establish
a centre at the polytechnic for very bright mathematicians
from middle schools and for their teachers, some of whom
might not be specialist mathematicians.

Children with particular talents are sometimes overlooked
in schools. But local authorities are increasingly using standard aptitude tests for primary and young secondary pupils.
These tests, which are a form of IQ test, serve two purposes.
They show teachers what children can and cannot do. They
also provide an objective way of checking whether children's
regular class-work is as good as it should be, considering their
ability. They are not usually pass/fail tests.

147

Sales of tests are booming. The National Foundation for Educational Research, which produces some of the most widely used, sold more than three million copies of various tests in 1977. Thomas Nelson, one of the main commercial publishers of tests, reported doubled sales in 1977–8.

Lancashire test the English and maths of nine- and thirteen-year-olds. Hampshire test nine-, eleven-, and thirteen-year-olds for general ability. Leeds test reading at eleven. Coventry were, in 1978, engaged in sticky negotiations with teachers' unions over cognitive ability tests for all twelve-year-olds and proficiency tests for fourteen-year-olds.

Teachers are wary of the growth of such testing. It smacks of the 11-plus and it represents interference with and questioning of their professional judgement. They have good reason to be cautious. Tests can distort teaching in the way the 11-plus did in some schools. Teaching can become concentrated on the skills needed to do well on the tests. This can severely limit the scope of schooling for all children and can be particularly disastrous for those who can do well in the tests without special coaching. Teachers may be encouraged to sit back feeling their job is done once they can claim to have got their pupils through the tests.

The effect depends both on the type of test and the use made of it. Testing has always been used in schools as a way of checking that children have mastered particular topics. The use of aptitude tests by schools is newer. In comprehensives, there is no sorting of children before they enter secondary school. If secondary schools are to extend all children adequately, they need to have some indication of their basic ability. The tests provide a useful diagnostic tool and a way of double-checking subjective judgements.

In a rather similar way, tests carried out by local authorities in all schools give them some indication of which schools are doing well and which are not. It is not necessary for this purpose to test all children in each school. Sample tests provide the necessary guidance. For it is when all children over a wide area are given standard tests that difficulties really arise.

Testing programmes on this scale are expensive, and there

a risk of the results being used not to diagnose the needs of individual children but as markers in a competitive race between schools anxious to attract the brightest pupils. It is this use of tests which most produces narrowing of the curriculum as teachers concentrate on the subject matter to be tested.

Testing goes with a growing attempt to coordinate what is taught in schools. The initiative has been taken by local authorities which have middle schools since secondary schools which take children only three years before O-level need to be able to rely on a rough uniformity in those coming to them. In the Isle of Wight, teacher coordinators on the authority's central staff have been working for several years to produce agreed syllabuses for main subjects. Guidelines, teaching materials and assessment tests were in use for maths by 1978. English, modern languages and history were under discussion.

In Leeds, the process was much further advanced. Teaching materials and specified 'targets' had been agreed in all main subjects and the authority's advisors were using the guidelines as a yardstick against which to measure the performance of their middle schools. The authority has an advisor who has been specifically charged with organizing the curricula of middle schools. They also have a large teachers' centre, housed in an imposing Victorian mansion and run by two ex-headmasters. The centre has provided a focus for much curriculum development work. It has also provided a centre for in-service training and, rather less officially, for keeping an eye on the city's teachers generally.

Progress inside even the most directive authorities is patchy. But the drift seems encouraging. The atmosphere of cooperation between advisors and teachers, in which agreed courses are hammered out, is markedly free of the strident protestations which greet any talk of nationally designed and imposed curricula. Something worked out by local teachers on their home ground has much more chance of acceptance than anything that could be prescribed or recommended from above.

Coordination between schools and toughness in running them were stimulated by former Labour prime minister, James Callaghan, when, in 1976 in Oxford, he made his first-ever

recorded speech on education. He successfully articulated th
widespread public anxiety about standards in schools. Th
speech coincided with increasing stability so that teachers ha
the opportunity to concentrate on the quality of their wor
It also tore away claims to immunity from public scrutin
which certain teachers' unions had sought to advance on be
half of their members.

Some of the reaction has not been generous. There ar
signs that growing numbers of children are being suspende
from schools. Though there are no national figures, and sus
pensions vary from a day or two to many months, Peter New
sam, London's education officer, felt strongly enough abou
the trend in 1978 to issue this warning in a speech to th
Howard League for Penal Reform: 'At the very momen
when conditions seem better than ever before for dealing wit
bad behaviour in schools, there are powerful forces drivin
the system towards intolerance.'

Schools, he said, were competing for a dwindling numbe
of children. Parents want good teaching and good discipline
Schools are therefore tempted to demonstrate their severit
and avoid the risk of disruption by hastily suspending childre
who are difficult.

Juvenile crime has been rising in recent years, and th
schools, as shown in Chapter 1, are not immune from suc
changes. But there is no evidence that the introduction o
comprehensive schools has had any causal effect upon delin
quency rates. What has happened is that clever children ar
now exposed in school to their delinquent peers in a way whic
is new. Michael Rutter's research (see page 135) shows clearl
that schools can, with good organization and a good atmo
sphere, improve both behaviour and attainment without tak
ing draconian action. This requires a considerable act of fait
and the confidence to convince anxious parents that their hard
working and well-behaved children will not suffer.

More constructive is the careful work now being done by
local authority officers and head-teachers to try to rais
teachers' expectations of their pupils – probably the most im
portant single factor in improving schools. If teachers' expecta

ons are high enough, it does not greatly matter what form of rganization exists either between schools or inside them. aising expectations is a massive and difficult job. In 1978, heila Browne, head of Her Majesty's Inspectorate, wrote in paper prepared for the first meeting of the reformed Schools ouncil, 'There is a fair amount of evidence throughout the hool system that pupils could do more than is asked of them.' a making this statement, she was drawing on the then un-ublished findings of the HMI survey of secondary schools ee page 165). It was widely recognized long before the sur-ey appeared that expectations were generally too low and that here is universal helplessness about how they may be raised. ne local authority officer, asked how his department could t about the job, simply shrugged his shoulders. 'I don't now,' he said. 'I was hoping you'd tell me.'

Reorganization has meant that, as Her Majesty's Inspectors ut it in their papers for the 'Great Debate' meetings :

Teachers accustomed to teaching only intellectually able pupils re now required to teach pupils of all abilities, including reluctant arners at all levels, and not infrequently to teach subjects with hich they are unfamiliar. On the other hand, teachers less well ualified find themselves required to teach pupils of higher ability an any they have met before.

In-service training for teachers is generally the solution sug-ested for adjusting expectations. It was widely reported in 977 and 1978 that local authorities were failing to use money llocated to them for in-service training. The amounts spent radually built up in 1978, and much of the effort was con-entrated on work inside schools. All over the country, meet-ngs and reappraisals, courses and discussions were going on. We discuss all the time – to the point of exhaustion.' 'Now we re able to turn to the clever children. So far we have con-entrated on the least able.' The same thing was said again nd again.

The National Association for Gifted Children, a private ressure group which has consistently campaigned for more ecognition and support in ordinary schools for children with outstanding talents, has found demand for information and invitations to speak increasing markedly.

Bristol University, as part of its training course for post graduate teachers, has for several years offered an option on giftedness which involved working with very clever children (IQ over 130) 'borrowed' from local schools for an afternoon a week. In 1978, a research proposal for a similar exercise at the Oxford Department of Educational Studies was approved.

The Inner London Education Authority published in *Contact* (9 November 1977), its own magazine – presumably for teachers' edification – the results of surveys carried out by D. S. Ramsden, among sixth and fifth formers and among teachers, asking about incentives. The teachers' answers suggested mainly such things as giving ample praise where it was due, removing disruptive pupils promptly from classrooms, less nagging and more interest. The pupils were tougher. Home work should be set regularly, collected regularly and marked regularly. The books should be better, tests given regularly at the end of each topic, the lessons prepared, and, 'They should make pupils work harder and stop them from wasting time.'

In Nottinghamshire, a special team of peripatetic teachers was appointed to start work in September 1978, going round the schools working with the most able children in whatever way seemed most appropriate.

In Devon, in 1977, a county study group published a paper of guidance for schools on spotting gifted children. The county has set up two centres to which primary-age children thus identified go for half a day a week for extra teaching or special projects.

The work is also going on inside individual schools. One School Z, in East Anglia, had in the autumn of 1977 just succeeded in phasing out what the head described as 'very boring worksheets' in favour of textbooks. He spent as much on his library as does Eton College (£3,000 a year). He had upgraded the craft subjects, which were compulsory for everyone, to include an O-level in engineering design. And he had nearly trebled the O-level passes with a stable staff, nearly all of whom were the original secondary modern staff before reorganiza

n. Their first Oxford entrant went there to read physics in
'8 – he was taught electronics by the staff in the lunch hour
d learned about lasers from a local university lecturer. 'Our
blem all along has been to get the pace up,' the head said.
the staff go 10 per cent faster and it works they think,
'ell that's great." There is constant pressure on them to
rease the pace. They find it quite astonishing. One English
cher who had been in the school sixteen years prepared a
son the other day on the difference between poetry and prose.
thin two minutes one of the first-year children had asked her
explain "poetic licence". They are just not used to bright
ldren. They expect to spend hours on a topic and then find
ldenly they're through it and out the other side in a few
nutes.'

As part of the process in this school, mixed ability teaching
d been totally rejected. The school was divided into three
oad bands by ability with three forms in each. All children
lowed the same course in the first two years (they came into
 school at twelve), so that all options could be open to every-
e in the fourth year. Maths, English and French were taught
 ability groups chosen from within the bands, and the top
nd and the bottom band were divided into four classes for
ost lessons. Economic cuts could make it impossible to con-
ue that for the top band.

Schools that do only CSE in the fifth year have been com-
g under pressure to provide O-level, sometimes from the
rents, as in the case of School J, sometimes, as in a much
ger girls' school in another inner city, from the pupils. In
e second school, the staff, resolutely committed to mixed
ility teaching and to CSE on educational and philosophical
ounds, were beset by pupils demanding more work and stay-
g on after school to study for maths and physics O-levels.

As the grammar schools and direct grant schools dis-
peared, schools like these, which were effectively secondary
oderns whatever their name, began to get more able pupils
nong their entrants. In one large inner city school, School
 with mixed ability teaching in the first two years, the
ogress of bright children was checked at special staff meetings

every term. Their work was compared with their primary records and their earlier work, and if they were not up scratch they were carpeted – and, by implication, so we their teachers.

In School H, where the mixed ability scheme caused wor a new deputy head was appointed with a brief to improve ac demic standards. Teachers who did not mark books or s homework were chased; one had even been formally rep manded. 'I believe in homework. The heads of departmer believe in it. Some of the staff do not. I encourage the parer to complain if not enough is being set.'

He was checking members of staff to see whether they we using appropriate methods for mixed ability groups. 'Of t tutors in the first year, seven are aiming very strenuously approach mixed ability groups with mixed ability teachir One I don't know about, two I doubt are.' He expected t staff to set different homework for children of different abiliti and to grade it not by a class standard but by how good it w for a child of that ability.

He had also been interviewing all the fifth-year childre 'Sometimes it's the first time they've had a reasonably long pe sonal talk with a member of the staff. There are too many ni little boys with white shirts and brushed hair who are gettir away with it. They are just not slogging their hearts out. these talks I can put the finger on them.' He recognized needed to be done earlier in their school careers.

In School J, the headmistress had in seven years welded t gether two warring secondary moderns, a 'nice' suburban or and an extremely rough one, which had, just before she w appointed, been hastily amalgamated on the same site. Wh she arrived, the school was chiefly known for its pre-eminen at producing shoplifters. By consultation, diplomacy a stealth, she had in 1978 got all her staff – 'Nearly all of the new in my time, thank God' – to agree to the introduction a standardized record-keeping system covering all departmen This followed on from the introduction of cognitive abili tests for the first-year pupils.

She finally succeeded in getting agreement by organizing

ies of workshops for all the staff – ten at a time for a whole
y. Among the discussion materials was a genuine case his-
y. The maths department had put a girl into a CSE group.
e wanted to train as a state registered nurse and needed O-
el maths. Her parents complained. The teacher and the
ad of the department were adamant. The parents produced
r school reports and contacted their Member of Parliament.
e reports were consistently excellent, all test scores con-
tently around 80 per cent, and the MP active. They got
eir way. But if they had not bothered to insist, that child
uld have been unable to take her nursing course on the
ength of one teacher's subjective judgement. 'The staff were
palled. They realized we simply couldn't go on with such in-
equate assessments.'

In School G, objective testing was not carried out as a matter
policy, but the philosophical zeal behind the decision was
ding in 1978 when a new deputy head replaced the one who
d moulded the school's policy. A symptom of the change was
e general agreement when one head of department said, 'I'm
t worried about those who want to succeed. But I am
rried about those who do not want to. They have the wit
d the intelligence to know that the system is too big to catch
em or to bother with them.' Children's progress and effort
ere being recorded meticulously in the school by every
acher, but only on a subjective basis.

At least to outside inquiries most of the staff were supremely
nfident that this method of recording and their own pro-
ssional expertise were enough to ensure that they did not
iss bright children. 'You really must allow that the teachers
ave an element of expertise,' the school's head of guidance,
e man in charge of course and careers advice and internal
onitoring, said severely.

The head of School J, asked about this, took a pithy view.
hat's bunk. I've even got one head of department in this
hool – not to mention other members of staff – who is totally
capable of telling. They think the ones who are able are the
nes who are neat and tidy.' She had put one of her deputy
eads in charge of the school's resources centre. All work-

sheets went to her for reproduction. Drawings were redraw
and the sheets checked for reading level and to see if they p
vided extra work for those who finished fast. At first a lot we
sent back to the staff for revision. 'It's not so necessary now.'

The number of initiatives of this kind has been growi
fast in recent years. Though undramatic and still expe
mental, they represent the first steps to improvement in t
quality of teaching for all children in comprehensive schoo
including the clever ones. Such programmes, because of the
piecemeal nature, can be underestimated. They promise mo
real improvement than do grandiose national schemes invol
ing yet more upheaval and structural change. They are tim
consuming and complicated and seriously threatened by cu
in services.

7 Summary and Conclusion

During the decade of the 1970s schools and local authorities have been in confusion and upheaval. The strains and pressures of school reorganization and local government reorganization have been compounded by a rapid expansion of the school population and rapid changes in social patterns.

In the process, the sort of children who would have passed selection tests at eleven have had their differentials of privilege and place eroded. They no longer have a monopoly of the most academic teachers; they no longer have the undivided attention of the school staff; academic values are no longer the overriding preoccupation of their schools; and suddenly they are a minority among a peer group which does not much value academic pursuits. In short, the clever are now only one part of a secondary school system which is specifically designed to foster the talents of all children up to sixteen. In the past, they were the main recipients of extended secondary education.

This diminution of differentials has brought an edge of fear and rancour into discussions of schooling, the more so because fear has been played on by those with a vested interest in preserving the bastions of selective education: the remaining grammar schools, the ex-direct grant schools and the independent schools.

Special pleading and aggressive lobbying have made it hard to assess objectively the merits of changes inside the new schools. New teaching methods, new ways of grouping children, new curricula designed to make what schools do appropriate to their whole clientèle, can easily be regarded as a threat and dismissed out of hand by people who did well under the old system. There is plenty of anecdotal evidence to support such contempt. The enterprise is new, the task hard and the realization often far behind the expectation. There is widespread anxiety about the future. In particular, it is feared that when the grammar school groups at the top of recently formed comprehensives leave school, and the remaining grammar schools vanish, there will be a collapse in academic attainment.

As yet no clear evidence exists of any collapse. Instead, there is evidence that a massive and dramatic disruption has so far done nothing to raise academic attainment at the top levels but has coincided with growing measured attainment at the middle ability levels. As comprehensive education spread in the 1970s the percentage of children getting five O-levels and two or more A-levels – for better or worse, the only measures we have of academic success in school – has stayed almost stationary. During the 1960s it had grown enormously. In the same years the proportion of young people leaving school with some sort of exam success has moved from under half to over four fifths. The top has stayed steady while the middle has expanded.

It is impossible to isolate the part, if any, that comprehensive schools may have played in producing this phenomenon. In the first place, the variation between comprehensives is at least as great as any differences between comprehensives and selective schools.

Secondly, comprehensives are new. Results apparent several years ago can hardly be attributed to comprehensive reorganization. Even in 1978, when over four fifths of all secondary children were in comprehensives, only about half of all fifth formers and a third of all second-year sixth formers had entered comprehensives at eleven.

Thirdly, comprehensive reorganization is even now less than complete. Six per cent of all children are in mainly selective independent and ex-direct grant schools. Another 7 per cent of the secondary population are still in grammar schools. A large number of so-called comprehensives are, in reality, renamed secondary moderns. The selective part of the system no longer has a proportionate share of dimmer children, the non-selective sector still lacks many of the clever.

Fourthly, and most important, the Certificate of Secondary

Education (CSE) was only introduced in 1965. And the school-leaving age was only raised to sixteen in 1973/4. Before that time, it did not coincide with the time of the first public examinations. The expansion of certificated attainment in the middle group occurred mainly after the leaving age was raised and now shows signs of stabilizing. It is mostly the result of these factors, just as the expansion of O- and A-level passes in the 1950s and 1960s was the consequence of an expanded field of entry as free secondary schooling became available to all after the war. This expansion of the field of entrants has gone hand in hand with institutional broadening of opportunities, but it is not possible to dub one cause and the other effect.

Absence of proof as to the effects of comprehensive reorganization, however, renders speculation free. And my hypothesis, based on scrutiny of the figures and the general rhetoric, and on impressions of the schools, is this: the cleverest group are no longer reaching the same level of detailed, disciplined academic work at the age they reached it before. At the same time, the middle range of children have gained self-confidence and certificated success in a whole range of courses, conventional and unconventional.

In some degree, the success of the middle group of children – and they include the old grammar C stream pupils – has been bought at the expense of specialist knowledge and early academic laurels for the old A and upper B stream pupils. Bright children are arriving later and by more haphazard paths at their qualifications. Those qualifications may well be broader, but there is a risk, too, that they will be in an unbalanced range of subjects and at lower grades.

School for these clever children will have been broader socially and often also in curriculum. They will have had the chance to develop non-academic skills to an extent that is now visibly forcing imitation upon remaining selective schools, be they grammar or independent. They may well have been bored, but they will not be burnt out. They may have been left to sink or swim according to their own initiative and that of their families, but they will not have been spoon-fed or crammed.

There is, in short, a changed emphasis in comprehensiv
schools which means that, by its nature, some of those wh
would thrive best on conformist, grammar school training ar
getting lost while others who, for whatever reason, would fai
to reach a grammar school or to flourish once there have nev
opportunities. And this is quite apart from the inexcusabl
loss of some children's chances in the chaos of reorganization.

The chaos is now abating, and there are everywhere sign
that schools are becoming aware of the price they have un
wittingly exacted from the able. But two main questions hav
still to be answered. The first is how much a slower pac
matters, how much these children gain other things on the way
and catch up academically later with relative ease. The secon
is whether their 'sacrifice' is a necessary condition for securin
the success of the less clever. If it is, whether it is worth while
and how much can be done to minimize loss without jeop
ardizing others' gain.

As to the first question, there are indications that academi
catching up is relatively easy given the chance, and there ar
many indications that other areas of endeavour are flourish-
ing as never before, thanks to the participation of the bright
School music has undergone major change in quality and
quantity. The art and craft facilities of comprehensive school
are more generous than those enjoyed by most grammar
schools, and the presence of these subjects on school timetables
means they are presented as useful and important skills rather
than as hobbies. Electronics, drama, swimming, dance and
gymnastics, poetry writing, community service, mountaineer-
ing – the list of subjects which are burgeoning is long and
wide ranging. They present much in the way of compensation
for slower pace; indeed, offer a richer prospect than narrow
specialization.

None the less, there is cause for concern. In the first place,
we are a relatively poor country with relatively restricted
access to a higher education system of unusually high pressure
and standard. We have a markedly stratified society in which
a secure and comfortable life, once largely dependent on birth,
is coming increasingly to depend on education.

We cannot easily afford to broaden and lengthen our higher education, nor are there signs of any pressing political pressure that we should do so on social or economic grounds. Yet a relatively fine selective mesh means that potential candidates for the élite are jostling for places, not just for any places in higher education, but for the most esteemed places, for the ancient universities and the courses leading to lucrative and comfortable professions.

Engaged in this competition, this country has, as well as its state schools, a private sector which is increasingly trading upon its ability to produce success in the race, and its willingness to undertake the job of preparing young people academically for highly specialized three-year honours degrees. Independent schools and direct grant schools, with under 6 per cent of all children, have a fifth of all A-level candidates and university entrants. Getting left behind at eighteen therefore implies a major risk. Furthermore, any real reappraisal of the value of a slower, broader school education runs foul of a set of powerful vested interests: universities who have come to depend on getting well-prepared specialists and schools expert in producing them.

There is further reason for concern, quite apart from external pressures, in that at least some of the holding back and lack of pace is not the result of a deliberate and well-arranged broader educational programme. It is the result of poor teaching, low expectations and bad organization. It is not all broad. Much is just boring.

As to the second major question, there can be little doubt that the presence of the bright, coupled as a result with postponing invidious labelling of the less bright, helps to boost both the morale and the attainment of those who would otherwise be seen to fail. If children are kept together, the brightest tow the rest at a faster pace. If children are not written off, they do better.

There can be little doubt, either, that a general raising of attainment is essential. This country requires less and less unskilled people, more and more who are skilled. We have an ageing population, and we have a complex society. To support the former and to operate the latter, we need a more productive and effective working population. It is of crucial national importance that as many young people as possible become productive, as few as possible become dependent. It is not a vast number more academics – or even a vast number more Nobel prizewinners, excellent as they are for national morale – that we need. We need versatile, practical people, capable of managing their lives, contributing to the lives of others, earning their living and enjoying their leisure.

The answer is not, therefore, to unpick the comprehensive system or even substantially to modify the principle, reverting to an older, academic approach. Postponing selection and segregation seems to offer the best chance of achieving what is needed. And even if it did not, there are no selection methods available which can be used with any reliability at all to sort out into separate groups the wide range of potential skills required to meet national needs. IQ tests of the 11-plus kind were already discredited for their manifest arbitrariness and error when they were used to select the top 20 per cent in academic terms. Between 20 and 25 per cent educated to a high level is no longer anything like enough, and academic skills alone are too narrow a basis on which to build a sound industrial nation.

Whatever the general democratic view, however, we live in a society which affords the individual a laudable measure of freedom. One of the characteristics of the bright and articulate is that they are good at looking after themselves. However beneficial the presence of the clever is to the less clever, it would be intolerable, impossible and unwise to force them to stay with the less clever if, in doing so, they suffered serious harm. We cannot after all do without high levels of achievement. And unless these can be fostered within the common schools, the bright will rightly leave when and how they can.

Happily, there are indications that, if children are kept together – at least in a general way – and the bright are at the same time encouraged to use and develop their capacities, they raise the levels of attainment generally and do very well themselves.

Attempts are now being made to see that this is done. There is a growing determination to give more attention to fostering the bright, a determination inspired in part by inclination and in part by a realistic recognition that the bright will not consent to stay unless something is done, and that if they do not stay the general task will be made very much harder.

Whether this determination will result in successful action, whether the apparent stagnation in achievement levels of the most able can be ended, whether, at the same time, the growing achievement in the middle ranges can be sustained, are very much open questions.

It is wholly unrealistic to expect that a high-quality mass education service can be run successfully as cheaply or as easily as can a system which nurtures only a relatively few chosen for their aptitude. It is wholly unrealistic, too, to expect all teachers to be specially gifted. The demands have to be tailored to people's real rather than imagined capacities.

To make the thing work, money as well as people of higher calibre are going to be needed. And the job they are asked to do – and, indeed, required to do – must be rather more clearly defined. Ways have to be worked out of grouping and organizing children so as to use the skills which any given set of teachers possess. Enormous ingenuity and care will be needed to see that the gains and losses are prudently balanced. Intricate monitoring and recording methods are essential – and useless unless efficiently organized.

It is not a question of testing and prescribing since standard procedures of this kind can never be designed for the top abilities. They tend instead to concentrate attention ever more on the average to the detriment of those who fulfil normative requirements with ease.

Gearing up the school system to higher levels of achievement will not be possible unless there is a general public and political will to make a success of what is being attempted. Things are not necessarily worse because they are different. Standards have not necessarily fallen because more people attain them. Erosion of differentials is not, of itself, cause for remedial action if the gaps were unwarrantably wide before.

Life is not over and the die irrevocably cast when a child is sixteen.

The purpose of this small book, as reasoned a polemic as I can make it, is to urge upon schools the need for more attention to the able, both for those children's sake and for the sake of the schools in general and all the children in them. It is to urge on politicians and administrators the need for clear-sightedness and firmness. But it is also to urge upon a more general readership some understanding of the task schools face, some appreciation of their successes and some generosity in assisting their efforts.

The task is hard. It is made infinitely harder by setting up alternative systems to 'save' the clever by taking them out of the common schools. The problem may appear to have been solved by such means, but it will not have been. Attention will simply have been diverted from undertaking the detailed, painstaking work that raising standards for all requires.

Appendix

Since the main text of this book was written, Her Majesty's Inspectors' survey of secondary schools, *Aspects of Secondary Education in England* (HMSO, London, 1979) has been published. It is by far the largest survey of secondary schools ever carried out in this country, and gives a detailed snapshot of the last two years of compulsory education in state schools.

The inspectors visited one secondary school in ten, comprehensives, grammar schools and secondary moderns. They concentrated on the last two years, and on maths, English, science and social and personal development in particular. Their report, widely expected to reveal a dismal picture of ill-disciplined schools where too little hard work was going on, was certainly critical but not in the ways that had been expected.

The inspectors found that few schools were characterized by bad behaviour, but that, on the contrary, most were hard-working and supportive communities with much solid work to show. The worst problem in terms of behaviour was absenteeism among pupils condoned by their parents. Nor did the inspectors find teachers wasting their time in the staff room or indulging in ill-defined progressive teaching programmes which neglected basic skills. They found, instead, teachers with too little time to plan courses and discuss schemes of work and children's progress with their colleagues. They found, too, much traditional, didactic teaching with dictated notes, set essays and the mechanical repetition of routine exercises, designed specifically to help children pass all-important public exams. They found too few books, laboratories, ancillary helpers and, above all, qualified specialist teachers.

In these final two years of compulsory schooling, the inspectors found that public exams, so much sought after by parents and pupils, dominated everything else. While this meant that the more able children were at least reasonably catered for, since the exams are designed for them, the less able were spending much of their time following courses which were not suitable.

In nearly all schools, public pressure had led not only to nervous pursuit of exam passes but also to a bewildering proliferation of options at fourteen. To satisfy public demand that schools prepare young people for adult life in general, a whole plethora of courses had, they found, been added to the basic academic, grammar-school curriculum. The result was often a bewildering confusion which made it hard for teachers to keep track of individual children. It was difficult in some schools to ensure that pupils followed a balanced course of study and were taught at a level appropriate to their ability.

Apart from the drawbacks of narrow teaching styles too deliberately focused on exam preparation, the inspectors found that, for the able, the academic load was often too heavy. Many of the brightest children were taking nine, ten or eleven O-level subjects. This meant that their education was unduly academic, squeezing out creative and social studies and depriving them of time to read around their subjects, to follow up practical applications and to discuss with their teachers.

The highest praise in the report is reserved for tough-minded, progressive teaching. Detailed assessment and preparation, challenging projects related to real life and involving cooperative skills of the sort used in adult life, courses of study which put basic skills to practical use are singled out for commendation.

The report highlighted the differences in staffing between grammar, comprehensive and secondary modern schools, with the grammar schools much better provided with experienced graduate teachers than comprehensives, and the secondary moderns very ill-supplied. Given this difference, it was striking that the grammar schools did not apparently do markedly better than comprehensives in the areas picked out by the inspectors as critical. Grammar-school teachers were found to be rather less willing to question the appropriateness of courses and were often failing their less able pupils.

Taken as a whole, the report sketched an ideal of a balanced, liberal education with strong links to applied skills. The means of achieving this suggested by the report lay mainly in the hands of the schools themselves with the leadership of the head teacher being the most important single factor. Weaker teachers were in particular found to be teaching in a narrow, didactic way through insecurity. In-service training and sound coordination and leadership inside the school could, it was suggested, do much to improve matters. Over time, the recruitment of more qualified teachers in subjects where there were shortages would, it was hoped, make further improvements possible. Rethinking courses for the upper secondary school would, the inspectors said, be stimulated by the introduction of the combined system of examining at 16-plus.

Published just seven months after the election of a Conservative government pledged to cutting public spending and improving standards in schools, the HMI report cut clean across the conventional wisdom of the Conservative party. Reliance on academic examinations, on strict discipline and on traditional teaching methods, the ideas put forward by many Conservative spokesmen, were in clear conflict with the inspectors' more expensive recommendations.

It was with this conflict unresolved that the new Secretary of State for Education, Mark Carlisle, embarked in late 1979 and early 1980 on an exercise designed to achieve some nationally agreed formula for the secondary-school curriculum: a framework which would set out what should be offered to all children in all schools. How liberally this framework should be defined, how success in achieving its requirements should be assessed, how far detail should be left to the schools and local authorities, how much of a pupil's time should be prescribed in this way all remained open questions.

Bibliography

The Attainments of the School Leaver, Tenth Report from the House of Commons Expenditure Subcommittee on Education, Arts and the Home Office, HMSO, London, 1977.

Benn, Caroline, and Brian Simon, *Half-Way There*, Penguin Books, Harmondsworth, 1972.

Black Paper 1977, edited by C. B. Cox and Rhodes Boyson, Temple Smith, London, 1977.

Braun, Carl, 'Teacher Expectation: Sociopsychological Dynamics', *Review of Educational Research*, Spring 1976, vol. 46, No. 2.

Central Services Unit for Careers and Appointments Services, annual bulletins, Manchester.

Comprehensive Education, Report of a DES conference, December 1977, HMSO, London, 1978.

Curricular Differences for Boys and Girls, education survey, Department of Education and Science, HMSO, London, 1975.

Dale, R. R., and S. Griffith, *Down Stream – Failure in the Grammar School*, Routledge & Kegan Paul, London, 1975.

Department of Education and Science, *A Language for Life*, Report of the Committee of Inquiry (the Bullock Report), HMSO, London, 1975.

Education in Schools, Green Paper, HMSO, London, 1977.

Enquiry into the Flow of Candidates in Science and Technology into Higher Education (the Dainton Report), HMSO, London, 1968.

External Influences and Pressures on Secondary Schools, County of Avon Education Service, 1977 (typescript only, not commercially published).

Fifth and Sixth Formers' Attitudes to School, Work and Higher

Education, a survey by Gareth Williams and Alan Gordon commissioned by the DES (mimeo form only). Extracts published by *The Times Higher Education Supplement*, 27 February 1976.

Fogelman, K. R., *Britain's Sixteen Year Olds: Preliminary Findings from the Third Follow-up of the National Child Development Study* (1958 chort), National Children's Bureau, London, 1976.

Future Trends in Higher Education, HMSO, London, 1979.

Gifted Children in Middle and Comprehensive Secondary Schools, HMI Series, *Matters for Discussion*, No. 4, HMSO, London, 1977.

Hampshire Education Committee Handbook, *Mixed Ability Grouping in Secondary Schools*, May 1977 (not commercially published).

Headmasters' Conference, *Report on Modern Language Teaching*, HMC, London, 1976.

Heim, A. W., and K. P. Watts, 'Comparison of Tests AH2/AH3 with Academic Criteria', *Research in Education*, No. 18, 1977, University of Manchester Press.

Her Majesty's Inspectorate, *Behavioural Units: A Survey of Special Units for Pupils with Behavioural Problems*, Department of Education and Science, HMSO, London, 1978.

Her Majesty's Inspectorate, *Truancy and Behavioural Problems in Some Urban Schools*, Department of Education and Science, HMSO, London, 1978.

Higher Education into the 1990s: A Discussion Document, HMSO, London, 1978.

Hilsum, S., and C. R. Strong, *The Secondary Teacher's Day*, NFER, Slough, 1978.

Hoyle, Eric, and T. Christie, Second Report of the Public Schools Commission, Appendix 5, HMSO, London, 1970.

Hoyle, Eric, and J. Wilks, for the Department of Education and Science, *Gifted Children and Their Education*, HMSO, London, 1974.

Industry, Education and Management, a Discussion Paper, Department of Industry, London, 1977.

Lobascher, M. E., and N. P. C. Cavanagh, 'The Other Handicap: Brightness', *British Medical Journal*, No. 2, 1977.

Mathematics, Science and Modern Languages in Maintained Schools in England, an appraisal of problems in some key subjects by HM Inspectorate (not commercially published), DES, London, 1977.

Ministry of Education, *Half Our Future,* a Report of the Central Advisory Council for Education (England) (the Newsom Report), HMSO, London, 1963.

Mixed Ability Work in Comprehensive Schools, HMI Series, *Matters for Discussion,* No. 6, HMSO, London, 1978.

Modern Languages in Comprehensive Schools, HMI Series, *Matters for Discussion,* No. 3, HMSO, London, 1977.

Neave, Guy, *How They Fared,* Routledge & Kegan Paul, London, 1968.

Primary Education in England, a survey by H.M. Inspectors of Schools, HMSO, London, 1978.

Pringle, M. Kellmer, *Able Misfits,* Longman, London, 1970.

Report of the Ministers of Education's Central Advisory Council, *Early Leaving,* HMSO, London, 1954.

Rutter, Michael, Barbara Maughan, Peter Mortimore, Janet Ouston, with Alan Smith, *Fifteen Thousand Hours,* Open Books, London, 1979.

School Examinations (the Waddell Report), HMSO, London, 1978.

Snow, Lord, *The two Cultures and the Scientific Revolution,* Rede Lecture, Cambridge University Press, 1959.

Ten Good Schools, HMI Series, *Matters for Discussion,* No. 1, HMSO, London, 1977.

Walker, David A., *The IEA Six Subject Survey: An Empirical Study of Education in 21 Countries,* Almquist & Wiksell, Stockholm; John Wiley & Sons, Chichester, 1976.

Whitburn, Julia, Maurice Mealing and Caroline Cox, *People in Polytechnics,* Society for Research into Higher Education, University of Surrey, 1976.

Willmott, Alan, *CSE and GCE Grading Standards: The 1973 Comparability Study,* Schools Council Research Studies, Macmillan, Basingstoke, 1977.

Yates, Alfred, and Douglas A. Pidgeon, *Admission to Grammar Schools,* NFER, Slough, 1957.

Statistics: Figures are taken from Department of Education and Science published statistics in most instances. Some figures were, however, supplied to me direct by the DES in response to particular questions, and I am most grateful for their help. University figures are taken mainly from the Universities Central Council for Admissions published figures or from the Final Report 1978 of the Conference of University Administrators Group on Forecasting and University Expansion (available from CUA, University of East Anglia, Norwich). Figures for individual schools, local authorities and universities have generally been given to me on request, though most of the figures for Cambridge are published in the *Reporter* annual admissions bulletins and for Oxford in the *Gazette* annual admissions bulletins. Again I would like to thank for their help all those who supplied me with figures.

More About Penguins and Pelicans

Penguinews, which appears every month, contains details of all the new books issued by Penguins as they are published. It is supplemented by our stocklist, which includes almost 5,000 titles.

A specimen copy of *Penguinews* will be sent to you free on request. Please write to Dept EP, Penguin Books Ltd, Harmondsworth, Middlesex, for your copy.

In the U.S.A.: For a complete list of books available from Penguins in the United States write to Dept CS, Penguin Books, 625 Madison Avenue, New York, New York 10022.

In Canada: For a complete list of books available from Penguins in Canada write to Penguin Books Canada Ltd, 2801 John Street, Markham, Ontario L3R 1B4

In Australia: For a complete list of books available from Penguins in Australia write to the Marketing Department, Penguin Books Australia Ltd, P.O. Box 257, Ringwood, Victoria 3134.

Pelicans aim to offer a whole range of expert reading for the amateur reader. The following pages offer a selection from our recent and forthcoming publications.

Eurocommunism: Myth or Reality?

Edited by Paolo Filo della Torre, Edward Mortimer and Jonathan Story

Is Eurocommunism a sop to the West, and underneath, the same Stalinist wolf in sheep's clothing? Is it social democracy – a sheep in wolf's clothing? Or does it represent a genuine and momentous break from Moscow by the European Communist parties?

The analyses here, each written by an authority on his or her subject, cover virtually every conceivable aspect of Eurocommunism in an attempt to sort the reality from the myths. Part 1 focuses on the national parties in Italy, France, Spain and Portugal; their evolution and present predicament. Part II looks at the international implications of Eurocommunism, the problems the parties have in common and those they pose for the superpowers and the rest of the world.

Children in their Primary Schools

Henry Pluckrose

This book is written by an experienced headmaster for those who are interested in primary education in England but have little recent personal experience of primary schools. It examines both the content of the curriculum and the philosophy which underlies it, pointing out the different values of rigid curricular requirements in fixed age-grouped classes and family-group teaching with freer timetables – and showing us how play and work are equally essential, can be equally educative, and in many cases are actually interchangeable.

The NHS: Your Money or Your Life

Lesley Garner

Is the NHS terminally ill?

It is obvious from the increasing frequency with which the NHS hits the headlines that it needs major surgery. In her calm and comprehensive study, Lesley Garner shows that everywhere – both at home and abroad, regardless of economic or political bias – there is an ever more impossible struggle between supply and demand.

The British Experience 1945–1975

'Peter Calvocoressi's book fills a gap which is of great importance. It provides a full survey of the period from 1945 to 1975 of British economic, political and, to some extent, social history, and will therefore give guidance to the young people to whom this period is unknown and usually untaught in schools. Just as important, however, it will reveal to those who have been unfortunate enough to live through the period just how hellish it has all been' – John Vaizey in the *Sunday Telegraph*

The Family, Sex and Marriage in England 1500–1800
Lawrence Stone

This book studies the evolution of the family, from the (to us) impersonal, economically bonded and precarious extended family group of the sixteenth century to the smaller, affectively bonded nuclear unit that had appeared by the end of the eighteenth century, and shows how this process radically influenced child-rearing, education, contraception, sexual behaviour and marriage.

'An indispensable chart to a landscape which it will take at least another generation of historians to examine with any precision' – Keith Thomas

Progress For a Small Planet
Barbara Ward

Pollution, diminishing oil reserves and the chasm between the rich and poor nations dominate our headlines. Some people claim such crises are insoluble, others that the new technologies hold the answers. *Progress for a Small Planet* accepts neither view, but shows how new attitudes backed by new, more conserving, technologies can take us beyond these crises. Barbara Ward outlines the planetary bargain between the world's nations that would guarantee every citizen the right to freedom from poverty and keep our shared biosphere in good working order.